# Totally From Left Field

## by

## Vincent Jenkins

authorHOUSE

1663 LIBERTY DRIVE, SUITE 200
BLOOMINGTON, INDIANA 47403
(800) 839-8640
www.authorhouse.com

First published by AuthorHouse 12/12/05

ISBN: 1-4208-9808-6 (e)
ISBN: 1-4208-6204-9 (sc)

Printed in the United States of America
Bloomington, Indiana

This book is printed on acid-free paper.

## When You've got to Go!

Artie tried not to look to conspicuous that night as he lightly jogged across the parking lot from the rectory of St. Andrew's toward the high school. He strained a smile at the couples and families passing by in their cars, the halogen head lamps momentarily spotlighting him. Damn, he thought. This happens every time Father O'Brien does the evening mass. Old windbag! Artie hoped the school's night watchman didn't spot him with all the traffic. It was 8:30 p.m. and the school was closed, but Artie had to go.

He reached the small side door that lead to gym, looked around to see if anyone was paying attention and then gave the latch bar a jiggle. As a true testament to the watchman's rumored alcoholic memory, the unlocked door silently swung open. Artie slipped in and guided the door shut so it would not slam. With a full moon shining through the door's window, he had no trouble descending the stairs that lead to the locker rooms. Bashing open the "Men's Locker" door with both hands, he ran straight for the urinals, his fingers frantically working down his zipper to pull aside the boxer shorts. Finally, the three Heinekins he downed before mass came rushing out with the force of a mini fire hose! Artie's great sigh of exhausted relief shook the shower stall tiles as it echoed through the room. It look almost 30 seconds for his bladder to empty, and when done he leaned his head against the cool white plaster wall. All done, ALL of it is done! Artie smiled at the thought as he zipped up and headed toward his locker in the adjacent room.

The ground windows near the ceiling let the moonlight sufficiently illuminate the area, so he had no trouble in maneuvering through the second door that was always left open. He knew the way blindfolded, courtesy of the many "drinking" games the baseball team played after a winning game. He opened the combination lock with the skill of a 1940's safecracker, and left around on the top shelf until he came upon his "thermos". Unscrewing the thermos while he sat on the bench, he emptied out 2 small plastic bags, one containing a Bick lighter and rolling papers, the other his treasured "Acapulco Gold" stash. Normally paranoia and the threat of discovery would keep Artie from even thinking of lighting up on school grounds. But that was all done with now. Another smile found it's way to Artie's lips as he prepared the joint. The Class of '76 completed graduation ceremonies last week; he was a free man! Next week he was off to Miami to visit his cousin Bert. Bert, who at 22 had his own apartment and half ownership of a motorcycle repair garage. "Bring your ass to Miami and work for me, holmes," Bert had written in his last letter, "and I'll keep you in booze and broads all year long!"

Yeah, Miami! That was the serious deal. He would work for Bert, eventually get his own place and take part time courses at a local college. The ultimate goal would be to start getting some gigs with local bands. Hell, he was a good bass player. Not 'bad' like Larry Graham, but with the right band he could grow. And he would be on his own at last, living like an 18 year old should! No more of this white man's church bullshit for his mother's sake. They thought he was going to spend four years at the community college, living at home. Fuuuccck that! Once in Miami, he was free and legal. Nobody could touch him, not his parents, not Father O'Brian, NOBODY. He snickered as he gave the lighter an exaggerated flick. Here's to all you mutha's he thought. He was about to light the joint when he heard the outer door swing open.

Artie froze! His thumb quickly released the gas switch on the lighter, extinguishing the flame. A thin sheen of sweat appeared on his foreheads as his hands worked automatically, placing the joint and equipment back in the thermos as his cars strained to identify the intruder. The footsteps weren't heavy enough to belong to the fat watchman, but yet they sounded familiar.

The soft tap of shoes echoed off the tiles of the bathroom, getting further from the lockers, Artie gently placed the thermos back in his locker, slowly and silently closing the door. Dammit, he thought, I can't get caught now! Images of Miami being flushed down a giant toilet filled his mind as he silently crept along the locker wall towards the bathroom. He could hear one of the stall doors swing open, followed by the rustle of clothes. Luck was on his side! And he was about to do just that, when two distinct sounds caught his attention. The simultaneous tinkling sound of urination and that of a woman humming.

What the hell was a woman doing in the men's room at this time of night?!? Even if the watchman let in a straggler from the evening service, the women's locker room was surely open. Or maybe the chick was waiting to give a BJ to the guy in the stall. But he had heard only 1 pair of footsteps. Overtaken with curiosity (and a voyeuristic urge), Artie kept moving along the wall to the edge of the bathroom entrance. The woman's humming continued even as the toilet flushed, and Artie's head peaked ever-so-slightly around the side of the bathroom entrance. What he saw in the shadowy moonlight was Father O'Brian shuffling out of the stall with his pants down by his ankles. Nothing too unusual, since Father O'Brian was a known klutz (he had even forgotten to turn on the lights). Artie did notice, however, that the priest had strangely slender legs for a man. It also looked like he was wearing those bikini underwear, usually seen on gay guys at the beach. Artie bit his lip to keep from laughing out loud. So old Father O'Brian was a little freaky! Dammit, he would have to find out <u>after</u> he graduated. Visions of potential psychological torture and blackmail danced in his mind until the female humming began again. His head spun in all directions, trying to locate the hooker before she spotted him. But the mysterious woman could not be seen.

Father O'Brian had shuffled over to one of the wash basins, flipping on the faucet and bending over to wash his hands. The sink was spotlighted by a bright pool of moonlight, and Artie was struck dumb by the sight of a pair of shapely, definitely female legs leading up a firm, round woman's ass in black panties! And when the humming began again, he realized that O'Brian was the source. Artie's head and shoulders were now poking around the corner wall, watching in dazed wonder as "Father" (or whatever the hell he was) O'Brian dried his hands, inspected himself in the mirror. He opened his jacket to reveal what looked like half a vest. The priest then grabbed the back of his neck with both hands, and pulled. There was the muffled tearing sound of velcro as O'Brian neck separated in-two. He then pulled his head off, just like Martin Landau in Mission Impossible! Gone was the classic face of the white haired Irish priest. In it's place was a white woman with dark, buzz cut hair and sharp, European features.

This was too much for Artie! He bolted for the adjacent main door, slamming it with his hands. But instead of the door swinging open it pushed back solidly, sending Artie sprawling across the floor. The big night watchman walked through the door, his eyes trying to make out the floored figure before him.

"Jeez, I'm sorry Edna," the guard said in a hoarse whisper. "I just came by to see if you wanted a lift home."

"What are you saying Jimmy"?, the woman's said as she rounded the corner. The priest's vest was draped over her shoulder, the O'Brian mask dangling in her left hand. Even in the shadows, her naked torso sported the curves of a mature woman. She quickly glanced at the now crouching Artie. "Who the hell is this?"

Before the confused guard could respond, Artie leapt from his position, aiming a body block right at his shins. Jimmy the watchman yelled in surprise upon impact, then in pain as his fat body hit the floor. Despite the pain in his shoulder and side, Artie rolled to his feet and bolted for the stairs. Instinct told him that whatever the connection was between the night watchman and the fake priest was a secret not meant to be shared. As he leaped 2 steps at a time, he heard behind him the familiar rattle of Father O'Brian rosary (or perhaps he should think "Sister" O'Brian instead). beads. Damn she's fast, he thought. But the exit was just a few more steps away. Once outside he would run the 5 blocks to the police station, where he would be safe. Just as he hit the top step there was a small whizzing noise, and suddenly Artie's feet became tangled and were pulled from underneath him. His right hand failed out for the railing, missing it by an inch as slammed spread-eagle on the stair landing.

Stunned and exhausted, Artie lost several seconds of reality. When he became coherent, he was on his back, looking up at the red wheezing face of "Jimmy" and the grim, pouting mouth of "Edna". He tried to move, and felt his legs and hands bound together by some small chain links. Looking down his chest, he made out the beaded cord of a rosary! He wanted to yell out his favorite cuss word when things went wrong, but found his lips were sealed by masking tape.

Edna smiled a nasty little smile. "That's right kid. All tied up and nowhere to go," she said sarcastically. She rose from her crouching position. Artie noticed that she now wore a "Grateful Dead" T-shirt and baggy blue jeans. "I know this one. No chance of conversion. Get the van, he'll have to disappear tonight. He's got a cousin in Florida the parents can't stand. We can arrange a vanished during travel scenario that should fit".

Jimmy had hefted his bulk to stand up. "Great. Then I'll just get the van." He took off his cap and wiped his balding head with a handkerchief. "I'm glad this sort of thing doesn't happen often, otherwise the cops could get wise". He walked to the exit and paused before going, pointing at the beaded chain that held Artie. "So long kid, that was a hell of a run, but I've never seen her miss with those things yet!" And with a wink and a tip of his cap, he was gone.

The closing thump of the Exit door echoed throughout the dark empty school halls. Artie was somewhat hog tied, the rosary wrapped around his and tied directly to his ankle. He had been silently straining against his bonds, but all he managed to break was a sweat.

Edna took a cloth out of her pocket and wiped his forehead. "No can do Arthur. Those beads are a custom made alloy, 200 pound test for situations just like this".

Artie flinched at her touch. She had used his proper name with the same pompous tone that "Father O'Brian" had always used. He wanted to scream, promise that he would never tell, but muffled nasal noises were all he could produce. What is all this, he wondered. Why?

As if she read his mind, Edna stood and learned against the nearby railing. She pocketed the cloth and took out another rosary set. She casually twirled the crucifix end, which made a slight whizzing sound. "It's like this Arthur. Outwardly, women were always second class citizens in the Catholic order. Oh, you have some progress with the various off shoots like the Protestants. But nuns always took a back seat to priest when it came to important decisions. But what the general public never knew, and must never know is that the while the sisterhood had increase enrollment in the last 70 years, the priesthood had a devastating drop in numbers. And of those who joined each year, over 50% dropped out or were dismissed. So rather than lose the whole ballgame, a plan was devised after World War II to disguise nuns as priest and fill the void until we could get the numbers up again. The Vatican had worked with the Allied underground for years, so creating false I.D.'s and the disguises were easy."

She paused, staring out the door window at the headlights of a passing car. Breathing a little sigh, she continued. "Thing was, we nuns discovered that we did a better job as priest than the real priest did! We were better parish organizers, better bookkeepers, and a damn sight better counselors. So when the Vatican decided to end the project during the 60's, a core group secretly continued. We've been the secret force keeping the parishioners coming back, a sort of firebreak against all that sexist, patriarchal bullshit that comes out of Rome." She smiled as Artie's eyes widened in shock. "Oh I know that may be a little stronger that "Father O"Brian's moderate sermons, but you can't jump start every backwater parish into the 21st century. We've been getting quiet support for years. People like Jimmy are a true God send. And let me tell you, I'll be glad to get back into the penguin suit when this gig is over! The women in this parish are horny as all get out!

Another set of headlights illuminated the door window, and blinked several times. "That'll be Jimmy," said Edna. She put away the rosary beads, and pulled small syringe out of the same pocket. Artie began flopping like a beached fish, crying through his gag. This was insane! It couldn't be happening!

Oh, shush up Arthur," Edna scolded as she removed the cap of the needle and gave it a test squirt. "We're not going to kill you exactly. You'll wake up in one of our South American missions with a new identity and a nice rap sheet that will persuade the local federales to find other accommodations for you, should you decide missionary life is not for you. You weren't exactly a bad kid, and we do believe there's hope for everyone. But we can't risk exposure just yet." She expertly placed a knee on his chest to steady him, and leaned forward ignoring Artie's whimpering, "Sorry Arthur, but when you've got to go, you have got to go!"

## Future News Items

**New York:** <u>Manhattan</u>: Last night's 7th anniversary of the Broadway musical "Miss Saigon" was marred by violence when 62 year old Charles Shiboygan of Massapequa Park opened fire on the performers with a M-16 rifle during the classic "evacuation" scene. Several cast members suffered gunshot wounds, while dozens of performers and audience members were injured during the ensuing panic. Shiboygan, an actual veteran of the Vietnam war, was disarmed and wrestled to the floor be several stunned audience members who shared the balcony area with him. He was held until police arrived and arrested him. He is being held at the 23rd Precinct pending psychological evaluation.

32 year old Thomas E. Muffin of Brooklyn was sitting next to Shiboygan last night. He described Shiboygan as "Sweaty and nervous" from the opening curtain. "The guy kept fidgeting, muttering on about "Charlie's coming", said Muffin. "Then he screams 'In-coming', pulls this machine gun from under the poncho he was wearing and starts blasting. The audience thought it was a new addition to the show until one of the wounded cast members screamed, "Run you fools, that crazy fucker is trying to kill us!"

When questioned as to how a man wearing military fatigues, helmet and poncho was allowed into the theater during a dry summer night, a representative of the theater management was quoted as saying, "Hey, it was a slow night and he had a ticket, ya know".

**Minnesota:** <u>Minneapolis:</u> The Episcopal Church of the United States has filed a counter – suit against the Westin Hotel chain today. They claim public slander by the Hotel via a statement on local television earlier this month. That was when Hotel manager Alphonse Clamato announced that the Westin would no longer accommodate any Episcopalians for their future triennial religious conventions. Clamato claimed in his statement, "Every three years they come here and it's a "my room or yours" orgy. I can't tell you how many sheets we've had to burn. The other guest can't get to sleep and are harassed when they complain. Hell, these people are worse than the B'nai B'rith. At least they tip!"

A spokeswoman for the Episcopalians claims that Clamato is just trying to cover-up for his massive losses in a all night poker game with the Presiding Bishop, where she alleges that Clamato used "company money". A court hearing will be on the first of this month.

**International:** <u>Geneva:</u> Today the Swiss government has announced that it will no longer accept money from American Republican politicians and religious evangelist for bank deposits, and will subsequently be closing all present accounts. Noted for it's strict confidentiality, the famous "Swiss bank account" has for generations been used by international businessmen, criminals, warring nations, and just about anyone who has a sizeable income that they don't want the local tax man to find out about. When asked during a press conference why such a drastic, unprecedented move, government representative Hans Brinker said, "You know, we've held money for the Nazi's, the Mafia, drug dealers, arms dealers, dictators; but after what those sleazy bums did to their own people in the last twenty years, we just couldn't live with ourselves anymore". When it was pointed out that this could cause damage to the Swiss credibility, Brinker responded, "Hey, we're not giving out names, and we're returning every penny. How they explain all the money to their own government is their business. And they can kiss my Swiss ass if they don't like it!"

In a related story, the Republican Party has announced that for years many House Representatives and Senators have given "private consultation" to "various" corporations prior to their political careers, and are expecting large back-payments within the next few weeks. Details will be given at a press conference this Friday.

**Washington:** <u>Capitol Hill:</u> In a stunning move, the House and Senate unanimously passed new legislation that would eliminate all welfare reform legislation and return the system to a "1960's mode. House Speaker Newt Gingrich, vacationing at his summer home in Oregon, explained with uncommon frankness, "We fucked up. We didn't realize that to pull all those people to work would mean changing the entire economic structure. Overall management would have to take a wage and benefit cut, and a fair and equal business practices and jobs would have to established for minorities and women above the poverty line. Add to that getting rid of slum lords, tax dodges, monopolies and improving the educational system, it was just too much. The entire system as we know it would have to change. Shit, rich WASP male Americans just weren't going to stand for that!

**California:** <u>Venice Beach:</u>  The first annual "GNC Muscle Up" contest was cancelled yesterday when it was discovered that one of the finalist was not taking any anabolic supplements.  George "No Shit" Armstrong was suspected of not using any of the products distributed by the General Nutrition Center company when his muscle mass was measured in normal ratio to his body weight and height.  A spokesman for GNC stated that Armstrong is a body building anarchist who promotes "all natural foods and insanity like that" for body builders.  The contest will resume just as soon as all the contestants can be verified as GNC product users.

**Hollywood:**  Spokesmen for the Reconstructive & Plastic Surgery wing of Long Island Jewish Hospital in New York say that singer Michael Jackson condition, though no longer critical is "still guarded".  This following the pop icon's extraordinary incident during the Japan leg of his "Greedy M.F." World Tour.  Last week while on stage in Tokyo, Jackson was performing one of his famous spinning dance steps when he literally came apart at the seams and collapsed.  One eyewitness described it as "…like the scene from 'The Mask' where Jim Carrey changed into the crazy guy.  Only this time pieces of Michael kept flapping off and he was screaming and stuff.."

According to Dr. Chet Pleeze at L.I.J. hospital, Jackson had contracted a severe form of Asian flu which weakened his entire system.  "Given the stress of performing and lack of proper rest, Mr. Jackson's skin just couldn't keep hold of all his past plastic surgery treatments," the Dr. said.  Though no word was given as to when a surgical team would start putting him back together again, the hospital staff says Jackson is in good spirits.

Family members and Jackson's management team held a small press conference last night to assure the worldwide fans that their pre-purchased tickets would be honored, and the concert tour "Will only be set back by 3 weeks, tops".  Sources close to the family say that's the amount of time it would take for Janet Jackson to have her implants removed, take a few male hormone shots, and learn the routines so she can fill in for Michael.

------------------------------------

It came as no surprise today when Paramount Studios announced the production shut down of it's latest Star Trek movie.  Studio spokesman Ford D. Money cited lack of public interest, script and casting problems as reason for canceling the project.  "We had one surviving member from the original TV series that was so old he couldn't shit straight much less act," said Money.  "We also lumped together other cast members from the other two series, but it didn't help.  Out polls showed that people fell asleep just reading the potential script ideas.  Let's face it, how many times can you watch some jerk yelling Red Alert and pushing buttons?"

------------------------------------

World renowned director/producer Steven Spielberg was arrested by Federal Marshals today on charges of distribution of indecent material.  The charges stem from the opening of Spielberg's latest release "Walter and Me" which opened at local theaters without preview by critics, studio heads, or distributors. The film deals with Spielberg's "dream fantasy" of meeting his idol, the late Walt Disney. Apparently, one disturbing sequence involves Disney, Spielberg, and a anatomically correct Mickey and Minnie Mouse. "Despite amazing special effects, 90% of the viewing audience were sickened by the perverse acts depicted on the screen", stated FBI agent Hans Upp. Spielberg is being held without bail pending a trial date.

------------------------------------

Actor Robert Dinero is reported to be in good condition today following a near drowning during the recent filming of "The Story of Jesus". The chameleon like actor's concentration was broken during the "walk upon water" scene when a stage hand came down with a severe case of stomach flu. "I tell you, when Bob gets into a role, he goes whole hog," stated director Tobe Hooper. "When Bob said he could do the scene without special effects, I thought he finally flipped. But he went to Jerusalem and studied scripture for a year, then spent 2 years with Tibetan monks meditating for this, and to have the scene blown by some guy fart'in is a damn shame. Son-of-a-bitch almost made it!"

------------------------------------

**National:** A Federal law enforcement SWAT team was called in yesterday to storm the Los Angeles court room of the O.J. Simpson trial and "put an end to that nonsense", according to State Attorney General Janet Reno. The Federal agents arrested Judge Ito, the entire Defense and Prosecution teams and Mr. Simpson. While the Defense and Prosecution teams and Judge Ito will be thrown in jail for "contempt of the judicial system", all evidence and witnesses will be rounded up and flown to Switzerland for what Ms. Reno says will be "a trial by people who treat everything like a God damned watch. They take it apart and put it together to make it work right."

Though the action has been hailed and approved by Congress, legal, social and ethical experts around the country stormed the White House by letter, telephone and television demanding that President Clinton reverse in what activist Al Sharpton (who appeared unannounced and uninvited on ABC Nightline) "a horrible miscarriage of justice. Hell, they're carrying it right out of the country!"

In a related story, unbelievable witness for the prosecution Mark Fuhrman, the former Los Angeles detective and silly witness for the defense Kato Kaelin, former moocher, have both relocated to Saudi Arabia, were they have been granted political asylum and lucrative jobs on their local television. Both are said to be doing well and "laughing their asses off".

------------------------------------

On a sad note, Playboy magazine founder Hugh Hefner died last night, the result of a freak accident during a party at the famed Playboy Mansion. Reports from the local coroner and eye witnesses say that the Hefner's head became wedged in the cleavage of Playmate of the Year Lulu VaVoom during a photo session. As he went to hug the 6 foot 2 inch Playmate, Hefner tripped and fell head first into her chest. Famed comedian and long time friend Bill Crosby stated that, "because of the low cut of the dress and the underwire bra, those titties were really tight. The more they struggled to pop his head out, VaVoom would get excited and breath heavier. Old Hef never had a chance." The coroner's preliminary report states that death was due to suffocation and severe cranial abrasions.

----------------------------------

## Counter – Culture

The following event should probably take place within the next 30 years or so. The scene is a typical pharmacy in Anytown, U.S.A. Enter an attractive, 40 year old caucasian woman dressed for a hot summer day. She goes straight to prescription counter, where a classic looking pharmacist (male caucasian, early sixties, balding, a little paunchy with black horned-rimmed glasses) greets her with a smile:

**Pharmacist (Mr. Billings)** – How do Ms. Eldrige! Hot enough for you today?

**Ms. Eldrige** – And then some Mr. Billings. Thank God for your air conditioner.

**Billings** – Yep, that unit's been here as long as I have. (pridefully) You can't beat American craftsmanship. Well now, what can I do for you today?

**Eldrige** – Well, I finally got a week of vacation time from that old miser boss of mine, and I was thinking of the Bahamas. Problem is, I just don't think the tanning salon and a new swimsuit will do. So I, ahh I thought that..."

**Billings** – (with a knowing nod of his head) Say no more Ms. Eldridge. I get a lot of these request this time of year. When do you leave?

**Eldrige** – About 3 days. Is that enough time? I don't want to be too drastic."

**Billings** – Plenty of time. Now let me just bring up your stats... (he sits on a swivel chair and pushes himself over to a computer console at the far right behind the counter. Tapping a few keys, the screen scrolls to a complete chart of Ms. Eldrige's medical history. Splitting the screen, Billings brings up an 'alterations' menu). "Now then", he calls over his shoulder. "Will we be going native?"

**Eldrige** – Oh, not even! I think that's so silly if you can't speak the language. (laughs) I can't even do the accent for English! What can you suggest?

**Billings** – (He studies the screen) Well, with your bio-chemistry, weight, etc... I'd say Castilian Spanish would be good, or maybe Cuban? South American would react well with the sun on the Islands.

**Eldrige** - (enthusiastic) Castilian Spanish would be fine. It should go great with my red hair.

**Billings** – Spanish it is. Just let me link up with your doctor on the net to clear this prescription. (He types a few entry codes and waits. A few seconds later, his console beeps and information begins to scroll on an adjacent printer. He tears off the sheet, stands and walks to the backroom. A few minutes later he returns carrying a small paper bag). Here we go. Just follow the instructions, and people will swear you were born in Madrid for the whole week. Now will there be anything else before I charge this to your account?

**Eldrige** – As a matter of fact..(she leans forward and whispers, even though there is no one else in the room) I lost a little more weight than expected jogging this year, and it would be nice if I could put it back…in one place you understand. It's just that these modern swimsuits require a girl to be so, aaahh bouncy.

**Billings** – (gives a knowing wink and waves his finger in mock admonishment). You youngsters today. Always trying to improve on perfection. As my grandfather would always say, 'Anymore than a handful…'

**Eldrige** – (blushing) Oh Mr. Billings! How you do go on.

**Billings** – (taking a small bottle from a shelf and adding it to the bag. He goes to the computer, types additional commands, takes the printout and staples it to the bag before returning to the counter) Now make sure you eat 3 squares a day and get at least 7 hours of sleep. The metamorph prescription is fast acting, so you may feel itchy while your cartiledge and skin pigments reorient themselves to the Spanish genes. The mammary enhancer is focusing some nutrient intake, so if you don't eat and sleep properly, you'll get light headed or nauseous. Just follow the prescriptions and have a nice time, you hear?

**Eldrige** – (grabbing the bag and practically dances toward the door) You know I will, Mr. Billings. Maybe I'll have one of those Caribbean romances. Take care!

Billings waves goodbye. As the door closes, a sly grin comes over his face. He walks to the back room and sits down at an old fashion roll top desk. He opens a drawer and takes out fat bottle containing large black pills. Shaking out a pill, he pours a glass of water from a nearby pitcher. "Oh you'll have a Caribbean romance alright. You silly little twit." Popping the pill, he quickly swallows a glass of water, then rest the glass on the desk. Leaning back in the chair, he closes his eyes and sighs. Within a few minutes, beads of sweat appear on his forehead. Suddenly his skin begins to darken, and the paunch of his stomach recedes. Hair begins grow in the former bald spots on his head. He spasms violently and groans like an old man with a kink in his back. Then suddenly, it's over. Billings stands and stretches. He examines himself on the nearby wall mirror. His hair is now dark, full and bushy. The facial features are smoother, lips and nose fuller looking; definitely younger looking. His skin is a rich Bronze color, and he is now lean and muscled. Though now loose fitting, his pants reveal a sizeable bulge in the crotch. Smiling with now perfect teeth, he takes off his glasses and tosses them on the desk. "Oh yes, Ms. Eldrige. Quite a romance indeed!" Billings laughs maniacally, as he grabs the desk phone, hitting the automatic dial button for his travel agent.

------------------------------------

### True Facts the News Media Won't Reveal
(all sources remain confidential)

- There is really no true value to the television show "Baywatch". And it's not really all that popular. It's all a scam by Dow Chemical. Since they lost a bundle on the silicone implant lawsuits, they made a deal with the producers to insist that 90% of the women on the show use their product in return for massive payoffs. Oh, in case you've read otherwise, David Hasselhoff has no talent. He's really a ninety year old man that sold his soul to Satan for fame and eternal youth.

- Because of the baseball strikes, sports entertainment executives have secretly been paying off large groups of people around the country to generate an interest in "volleyball". The fact that most sport viewers immediately hit the remote control the second a volleyball match comes into view has been suppressed through "phony" Nielsen ratings.

- Howard Stern, Don Imus, Bruce Willis, and Sylvester Stallone are really card carrying Republicans who donate big bucks to the conservative cause. They just like to pretend their hip, rebel type guys, but secretly belong to an organization called White Hollywood Organized Republican Entrepreneurs (W.H.O.R.E.).

- "Barney", (the hokey kids program featuring some dancing wussie in a cheap blue dinosaur suit) is really part of a sinister plot by several large conglomerates to control the minds of the future working populace. Notice that children exposed to this junk walk around with glazed eyes repeating such banalities as "I love you, you love me"; these kids don't have the slightest inclination to count, spell, or solve problems. This is deep subliminal programming that will prevent them from forming unions or asking for fair wages and medical benefits.

- The concept of mass production was an idea given to man by the Devil. This was translated from one of 'The Dead Sea Scrolls' and kept secret by The Vatican all these years. It seems that since the Devil couldn't count on corruption to destroy God's creation (you and me), he whispered in the ear of some assholes to create technological industries that kept producing more non-biodegradable products than mankind will ever need. The Devil figured we would eventually would sink in our own surplus (in the name of competitive profit) and/or destroy the environment.

- There has never been a shortage of any species of fish, despite what environmentalist and small commercial fisherman say. Scientist discovered years ago that fish could communicate with humans by using dolphins and whales as interpreters. It seems that they have developed a successful means of hiding from fisherman. As a result, dolphins and whales are being given an L.S.D. type drug to make them divulge the secret. Unfortunately, the drug just caused the poor mammals to commit suicide by beaching themselves.

- Nuclear power plants were never really necessary. Scientists realized 50 years ago that by genetically altering and breeding hamsters, they could supply all our electrical needs through simple treadmill driven turbines. Nuclear power plants are just a scam to make profit by building and maintaining the damn things.

- UFO's and aliens really do exists. Thing is, they've never been interested in this planet or it's inhabitants. They just use the Earth as a rest stop between galaxies, and screw around with people out of shear boredom. The U.S. government denies and covers-up UFO existence because they're too embarrassed to admit that we just aren't that important in the universe.

- There was never an oil or gas shortage in the United States. It was all a successful plot by well connected short people to get those "little foreign cars" manufactured here.

- Our newspapers are really recycled toilet tissue. This would explain the content of papers like "The New York Post" and "Daily News".

- As a result of high caloric diets and combinations of various chemical pollutants, scientist predict that by the year 2020, large busted women will be the status quo for America. As one source (an elderly chemist) from Brookhaven Labs put it, "Big boobs will be so common, Kate Moss will definitely become a sort of reverse Marilyn Monroe icon. I'm glad I won't leave to see it!"

- Genetic engineering will never become a reality. Research scientist figure that super smart children will examine the world situation and then devise a way to "get the hell of the planet Earth" as soon as their old enough to travel. As one doctor put it, "what's the point in investing all that time and money when they'll just leave home and never call or write? Kids!"

- The legendary giant ape men of the North American woodlands, known as Big Foot, was discovered years ago. They're now being trained for cheap labor to construct McDonald's restaurants in Mexico, Haiti and Vietnam.

- The Jackson Family, of music industry fame, are actually a successful cloning project of patriarch Joe Jackson by military scientest. Mrs. Jackson is really Joe's younger brother in drag, a successful front that has fooled the world for years.

# SAD, BUT TRUE!
By Vincent Jenkins

**Service with a smile!**

… If you live in the New York area and need repair service for your refrigerator, washer, or plumbing; it's better than a 50/50 chance your repairman will wear pants that showcase the crack of his flabby butt. This high standard has been kept for decades, along with a pre-requisite that the average repairman: (1) is between 35 and 55 years old (2) generally in poor shape, signified by heavy breathing through the nose and profuse sweating from carrying his tools from your door to the kitchen. (3) will want to shake your hand right after he has stuck his down your toilet (4) has a personal hygiene that defies current over-the-counter deodorants and mouthwash.

… If you like intense arguments with condescending salesman, then rush down to your local music store outlet. Stand in the middle of the store staring at the category signs with a frustrated grimace on your face. A yuppie like name tagged youth walks up to you and asks "Can I help you?" You state the name of the song, the artist and the year or release. You also state the type of music (say jazz oriented). The store rep replies (usually with some Valley Girl dialect) "Oh no! It's under New Age".

Now for the uninitiated, I'll explain. New Age is a term whipped up by some wimped out baby boomers in the Mid-West and Southern Coast during the 80's. These clowns; comprised of ex-hippies, mediocre musicians & artists, and a bunch of disenchanted Ph.D.'s; latched on to an old philosophy (based on an incorrect calendar) that mankind was entering the next phase of intellectual and spiritual enlightenment. They begin pumping out books combining Native American folklore, traditional chinese medicine, English witchcraft and God knows what else; claiming all were connected to the New Age. And since every era in American history needs a musical signature, New Age music was born! Well, not born but sort of borrowed. You see, anyone in America over 30 who listened to more than just the Top Forty can recognize bits and parts of every music form in America jumbled together to make the tedious "elevator music with an attitude" that is New Age (if you've survived Yanni or John Tesh concert, you know what I mean).

So don't waste your time arguing with the store clerk. Do what I do. Wait until there's no one else in that part of the store. Then take all the good CD's and tapes, move them to their "true" categories, takes the NEW AGE sign, flip it over and write BULLSHIT. Then replace the sign and calmly (but quickly) leave the store. Believe me, you'll be going a service for future mankind.

… One of the most important industries in America is responsible for turning decent, happy human being into emotionless zombies. Zombies that are quick to anger if they are forced to use any brain power higher than basic locomotion and speech skills. I refer to the fast food industry. If you don't believe me, just check out the eyes of the person saying, "Hello, may I take your order." We're talking motion detection here, not human recognition. If you'd place a tree log with hat & glasses in front of them, it would have a burger & shake within five minutes.

… Don't you just love the service you get on the telephone? When companies are going to get money out of you (a.k.a. phone sales), they have the most sincere, courteous operators to assist with any problem. But when you're getting something back (like why your insurance company hasn't sent that claim check) it's usually some dullard with a short attention span that gives you cryptic answers the C.I.A. couldn't figure out.

... I can't speak for the rest of the country, but in New York City there is an establishment that rivals the Mafia in ruthlessness and crime against law abiding citizens. It's called the electronic equipment outlet. Under various logos, these stores practice the time honored routine of lying to the customer. Whether selling a used "boom box" as a brand new stereo system, or charging $115 in repairs on your TV to replace a fuse that cost $.79 cents, it's like a hungry monkey promising to hold a banana for you and not eat it. You know you're going to get the shaft.

... Forget exercise! If you want to give your cardio-vascular system a good workout, hop in a New York City cab just after rush hour and pick a destination that over 20 blocks away cross-town. Make sure you buckle the seat belt before telling the driver you're in a hurry. I guarantee it's better than any roller coaster ride in the country!

... In the not too distant future, prostitution will become legal across the 50 States. This means that entire new system of federal taxation, legal and congressional representation will be created for the men and women who provide sexual services to total strangers. Imagine a CPA preparing a 1040A form for these people:

**Account:** You see Ms. Johnson, I just can't write off 100 custom made condoms as a business expense. If your client can't fit into any of the variety available on the market, then he should have paid for them himself.

**Ms. Johnson:** Damn! Well, what about the inflatable rubber hobby horse? I had to have that thing made in Germany and delivered C.O.D.

**Account:** Oh that's alright. We can just put that under "entertainment expense". Well, that seems to be about everything. Now there's just the question of my fee..?

**Ms. Johnson:** Sure thing honey! Up the stairs and to your left, room 4. Do you want the high school outfit or tupperware sales lady?


**For your own good**

Now an off-shoot of the previous category is the social service known as "consumer protection". Ideally, the federal government enforces laws that prevent private industry from ripping off the general public, via shoddy products, false advertising, and price inflation. In some ways, this is like the fox hiring the weasel to guard a chicken coup. Case in point: radio commercials for automotive sales. At the end of every new car advertisement there's a man with a low, monotone voice rattling off a list of "restrictions and variations" like he's wired on cocaine. He recites in 40 seconds a list that takes 1 minute 10 seconds to read. This mumbling is done so that you and I will know not to expect to get a car priced "as advertised" because we were told the fine print in the advertisement. Unfortunately, most people retain their childhood attraction for big, noisy, shiny things. So once we hear **NEW, CAR,** and **SALE** in the same sentence (accompanied by loud music), it's lemmings to the sea time at your nearest dealership.

... Did it ever occur to the Emergency Broadcast System people that they might be promoting heart failure in America? I'm sure that somewhere there's an old person who's pissed his pants because he missed the "this is only a test" part on the radio while napping; having awakened to that high pitched "BEEEEEEP!!".

… We have child proof caps to keep little kids from getting into medicines, protective factory wrapping to ensure consumers that no one has touched the product after it left the factory. Unfortunately, most people get high blood pressure from the sheer frustration of trying to open the damn things.

## The Good Old Days

If you're in your late teens or early twenties, then you must be sick to death of hearing older people tell you how great things were before you where born. It's a time honored tradition for a 40 year old to tell a 20 year old "I remember paying **half** for a **much bigger** candy bar when I was your age.." etc., etc. Now obviously some of these comparisons are true. But eventually you'll come across people who'll tell you that everything was better when they were younger; and you're generation just can't compare. Here are some facts to help you deal with these blowhards:

<u>SEX</u> – (I can't speak for women in this category, so their off the hook). You know the type. Late 40's, gray and/or balding. Flabby or fat, and accents every sentence with the word 'man'. To hear them tell it, **everyone** was fucking their brains out in 1968. All you needed to know was where the party was, and it was practically a done deal (if you scored some booze or drugs, so much the better).

Now anyone who has access to some historical film footage, newspaper photos, or a family album should just take a gander at all these "hip" folks. Despite the wild hair styles and outrageous clothing, you can still recognize the wimps, the geeks, and the clowns (yep, some things <u>never </u>change!). So if your story teller is just an older version of the buffoon in the photo, chances are his recollection of "great sex" actually involved a copy of Penthouse, his right hand, and some amazing Hawaiian marijuana.

<u>MONEY</u> – "Getting more for your dollar" is one of the more elusive great American dreams. So when people tell you that your dollar could buy better quality (or quantity) 20 or so years ago, you get a little depressed. Don't be! What these dopes fail to mention is that their take home pay 20 years ago was comparatively as cruddy as it is today. They also seem to have forgotten the little things like inflation and recession. Yes, hindsight is a wonderful thing unless you're looking back at an asshole.

<u>MUSIC</u> – Yeah, you've heard it all before! Rap/hip-hop is junk, Grunge/New Wave is a joke. All current singers suck. Anything past 1979 is garbage. This from the people who thought Heavy Metal, Punk rock, and the commercialized disco era were good stuff.

"By the way, if you really want to start trouble, go to a party or bar and mention to some white people that jazz is America's <u>only original</u> music form, and that all forms of rock are just derivatives of rythmn and blues. Oh, and blue grass/country is a direct relative of Scottish Highland music. Then tell some black people that 90% of the instruments used by their favorite musicians were created by Europeans, who also developed the sheet music and technology to produce the record. What follows is the equivalent of a room of 5 year old arguing whether there is a Santa Claus.*

**MORALITY** – Strangely enough, it's rare to find a middle aged person say that the current generation's social mores are better than theirs were. Instead, you hear "crime is worse, kids are out of control, people don't respect each other, etc., etc." Then extremist religious groups and ultra-conservative politicians start laying claim to "the correct way of life". What these great social critics don't realize is that these problems have <u>always</u> been with us. It just that an increased population makes them harder to ignore. Don't believe me? Then what the hell were "The Dead End Kids", Humphrey Bogart and James Cagney movies portraying? 1940's Lithuania?


## Reality

… Good doctors promote health and save lives. Good lawyers strive to protect the rights of the individual, making sure they get justice whether guilty or innocent. Both careers require years of training, intellectual concentration and sacrifice. Both give substantial salaries and benefits. And both are highly prestigious and respected positions in our society. Yet, some simpleton who can get on TV an tell a joke about shitting his pants during a wedding ceremony will make more money than God; buy and sell his own personal doctor or lawyer and become an international household name for decades to come. Kind of makes you stop and think, doesn't it?

… I can't speak for other ethnic groups, but for black folk there has always been a self made "requirement list" used to judge the mind set/worth of the individual. In other words, unless you were born poor (or still are) and lived in an all black urban neighborhood (or still do) you don't know what it means to a black man in America (a version of this exists for colored folk on the Atlantic Islands). This means that all the suburban Negroes are out of the loop.

OK, let's take this train of thought to it's logical conclusion: if you're not black, poor and sharecropping in the Deep South you haven't a clue what it is to be an African American; and if you're not standing on the fucking Serenghetti Plains carrying a spear and herding cattle, you're not an African. Period.

… After all those lofty speeches and tearful ceremonies, most high school graduates can look forward to a summer of alcohol driven parties and working the night shift at 7-Eleven. This will prepare them for a college career of alcohol driven study sessions and working the graveyard shift of some local bar & Grill. Which will prepare them for an adult career of working the graveyard shift at the office and alcohol driven weekends. Yes, higher education. For a challenging, better life.

… It's comforting to know that after a long, hard day of lobbying for stronger drug enforcement laws, the boys on Capitol Hill can relax with an alcoholic drink of choice at some famous Washington bar & grill. Yeah, like Nancy Reagan wouldn't get her ass kicked if she walked in saying, "Just say no" to a bunch of tired, cranky and drunk congressmen.

… No matter what the Department of Motor Vehicles does; new state-of-the-art computer/camera equipment: faster, organized form processing; better trained, courteous personnel; when you get that driver license photo it's going to look a DWI mug shot from the county prison.

… Nudists have enormous house cleaning bills. Figure it out. Your a nudist, naturally the majority of your friends are nudists. Between social gatherings, parties, poker games, etc., there are a lot of naked butts sitting on your furniture. So unless these folks use your shower every time they "use the facilities", renting that steam cleaner once a week is without question. Unless you like fragrant reminders of how many party guest your couch has seated.

... You consider yourself a nice guy. A people person. You're good to your mother, work hard to pay the bills on time, and are considerate to your friends. Everyone who meets you says you're fair and honest. It's part of your daily routine to keep in good physical condition. Yet with all these great qualities, every woman you pursue has dumped you for the following:

(1) <u>The little geeky fat guy with the lousy job</u> – because "he's cute and makes me laugh".
(2) <u>The bad boy</u> – because "he's an animal. I don't care about his other girls, just as long as he calls me when he gets paroled."

**In the World of Science...**

... The Loch Ness Monster will never be found. If it (or they) ever existed, they've been killed off in boating accidents with all the scientific numbskulls running around the Scottish waters. Even worse, it probably ended up in a can of Star Kist Tuna after being captured by a Japanese research submarine.

... These simple facts regarding nuclear power plants are usually overlooked by the people trying to shove the damn things down our throats: (1) when all is said and done, the nuclear power plant is merely a elaborate way of boiling water to run a turbine engine, which produces electricity. This is the equivalent of setting fire to your kitchen to roast a turkey. (2) Millions are spent devising & developing ways to contain tons of deadly radioactive waste products, which will corrode their containers when your grand-children are about 40. Think of it as saving all the garbage bags you'll fill until you're 65. Then leave it all in your will to your kids (3) The same companies that charge you outrageous electrical bills now will be the ones to set your rates under nuclear power. Get the picture?

... Advocates of the NASA space program say that eventually space exploration will benefit mankind with new technologies, raw materials and medical discoveries. What they don't tell you is that each rocket launch pumps enough pollutants in the air to choke a fair sized town to death. So I guess we'll need those new discoveries, because at this rate we won't have any clean air left to breath.

... The science of genetics hopes one day to eliminate such human failings as obesity, eye sight defects, cancer, etc. Now the real break through is when they can eliminate killer bad breath and body odor from appliance servicemen, and New York cab drivers. Or better yet, self flossing teeth. This would eliminate finding that annoying bit of meat wedge just as you're kissing your date goodnight for the first time.

... It's only a matter of time before behavioral scientist are slapped with a discrimination, unlawful detainment and abuse lawsuit by all those gorillas they've been training to be intelligent. The first hint of this on-coming legal proceeding will be when a doctor says in sign language, "Does CoCo want a banana?", and the gorilla signs back "No, bitch! Get me a beer and Cable hook-up or I'll snap your god damn neck!

**Things that you hate to admit are true.**

… We are all capable of becoming blathering idiots when approached by the opposite sex to some degree. Example: Joe Stud Yuppie – works for a major corporation. Has bank, car, apartment, clothes, the works. He knows all the moves, on the job and on the club scene. Yet, let Ms. Something Special come into his office. Showing just a tad amount of cleavage and thigh, she laughs at all his jokes and touches his arm just so. By the end of the day, Joe Yup has given her his apartment keys, vital information to company secrets, and a promise to rent his mother as a cleaning lady on weekends. He also has lock jaw from grinning like a fool for over an hour.

By the same token, let's look at Ms. Jane Secure Person – self employed and successful. Has the same possessions as Joe Yup. She only dates mature, secure, and intellectual men who can deal with "a strong, independent woman". Then, while visiting a friend, she accidently bumps into the carpenter who's doing repair work. And he looks just like those bare-chested guys on the cover of those romance novel. Within minutes, Ms. Emancipated is transformed into a shy, giggling school girl; who can't look Poster Boy in the eye while standing on one leg; twisting from side to side while fidgeting with her hands.

Another incidence of being "struck dumb" by love (or lust) is the fabled "home cooked meal". When the object of desire invites you over for lunch or dinner, the idea of possible sex jumps from the subconscious to interfere with your cognitive reasoning skills. In other words, you'll swallow the worst cooked food in history with a smile and a lie ("It's good! Different, but good!") on your lips.

… No matter how old we get, the best laughter is still the childish "suppressed laugh". Laughing during situations or in places we're not supposed to. Case in point, your house of worship. If you have not held back a grin or snicker during one of the following events, then you're either without humor or lobotomized: (1) hearing your priest, rabbi, or reverend loudly burp during services. (2) watching a pall bearer get a leg cramp during the funeral procession. (3) noticing that the father of the bride has his fly open during the aisle march. (4) knowing that you an at least 3 other guys in the groom's party slept with the bride. (5) knowing that the groom is so hung over from the bachelor party that he's still wearing that Mickey Mouse condom. (6) (For Catholics Only) watching people fall on each other like dominoes when the fat lady at the end of the Communion line trips.

… You can hate the director, you can despise the producer. The plot sounds idiotic. Every critic you respect has damned this work. But no matter how bad the reviews, if a movie has well built members of the opposite sex in numerous nude scenes, you're going to cough up the bucks and warm up the old VCR.

… If you're single, there is no doubt that your love life is in the toilet when you can confidently put Monday's underwear on Wednesday.

… Let's say the ban on cigars & cigarettes becomes the law of the land. So millions of people are saved from lung cancer and respiratory illness. The general population becomes healthier. Well, even more millions are put on unemployment (farmers, manufacturers, distributors, advertisers, etc.), and their going to be real cranky when they can't light up while going through the want ads. Think about it.

… You can talk all you want about the exploitation of the American working man by the "fat cats". But no matter how much you hate the wealthy class, when you stay at a good hotel on the company's expense, you hit that Room Service button for everything it's got!

… No matter how big a "jazz buff" you are; no matter how "off the corner" a brother/sister you claim to be when it comes to "soul music"; I defy anyone to tell me the exactly what the hell the words are to an Anita Baker song by listening only.

… If you're a parent of little one who loves to listen to a favorite children's record over and Over, and **OVER** again; you periodically hide the record and lie like a rug, saying "I can't find it baby. Let's put on a better record until we find the old one."

… No matter how much you deny it; there will always be a part of you that regrets not being a shameless bastard and sleeping with your prom date's sister when you had the shot.

… No matter how big and/or strong you are, when your girlfriend/wife is going through "that time of month" you suddenly find yourself peeking around corners and walking on tiptoes.

… When you run out of clean underwear on Wednesday, or have a chance meeting with a sexy lady while wearing a severely wrinkled shirt and 2 day stubble, you realize Mom was right about "neatness always counts" and pray you never have to admit it to her.


**Permanent Press**


America has been "The Great Melting Pot" for some time now. So logically we should all be use to one another. However, those nasty stereotypes born of Old World propaganda still march on in the hearts and minds of Americans. These are just a few absurd prejudices that you can catch on any TV situation comedy, major motion picture, or in speeches given by various congressional representatives:

Southern Exposure – Yep, seems regional prejudice is alive and kick'in. The second a Northerner hears a "y'all" or "you all", they automatically assume that the speaker is some doofy, shit-kicking imbecile whose sister happens to be the mother of his son. Interesting, being that in my lifetime we've had a few President's with some serious Southern lineage who ran the damn country during tough times. Also, since the majority of our food is grown in the South, you would think most Northerners would have half a brain not to piss off the people that feed them.

New York, New York – New York City has long enjoyed the distinct image of being the most corrupt, decadent, crime ridden metropolis in the 50 States (with Los Angeles running a close second). Now New York City (no picnic area by any means) is no worse than several other major cities around the country. The problem is, most New Yorkers secretly enjoy this reputation because people assume you must be the toughest thing on two legs if you hail from "NU YAWK". However, any clown with a little practice can do a classic Brooklyn accent. So, the folks in the Idaho bar may be interested to know that the loud mouth tourist from NU YAWK is actually from a quiet suburb called "Little Neck", and not "from da mutha fuk'in streets, know what ahh'm say'in?"

The Local Folk – In case anyone has forgotten, rent is due to a few groups of people that never actually recognized this land becoming "the United States". They go by various names; The Sioux, the Cherokee, the Navajo, the Hopi, the Blackfoot, and a hosts of others. As this is the age of political correctness, these folks have undergone an image change. Instead of being a group of interior, primitive, losers who can't recognize defeat and have become a burden to society; they are now a group of stubborn soreheads who hold a grudge and won't get with the economic program.  This change of view recently came about when a few Native Peoples pointed out that what little sovereign land the government left them was theirs to do **whatever they wanted sans certain Federal laws.**  So now a bunch of pissed off land developers, casino owners, oil men, etc. are screaming "foul" because a bunch of "Indians" beat them at their own game.  If Tonto were alive, he might say "Blow it out your ass, Kemosabe".

# Expressly Forbidden
## by Vincent Jenkins

As you go through life, you become familiar with the "unwritten laws" of society. Most people know and accept the "do's" of social interaction, because they make (for the most part) logical sense. It is the unwritten "do not's" that people have trouble with, as they can be misinterpreted or illogical. Let us do a quick examination of these acts that must **never** happen in public.

## The Human Body

- Sexually physical reactions in public: You can comment on how nice someone looks. You can even compliment a person on how attractive their date/spouse is. But you must never display sexual appreciation. This law is for men, because women don't have to worry about their pants resembling a circus tent if they get turned on. Oh sure, their nipples may pop up to say hello from time to time, but a cool breeze or a Johnny Mathis tune will get the same result. So women can pretty much cop a plea in this case, but men are defenseless. Probably in ancient times, an abdominal salute at the sight of someone else's wife or girlfriend would result in a fight to the death. So as we became "civilized", guys who were caught are either never invited to another party or are the subject of many childish jokes for the rest of their lives. Now really, how civilized can we be when at a twenty year high school reunion the winner of a Nobel Peace Prize is still referred to as John "Flag Pole" Wilson?

- Succumbing to bodily functions: Hey, when you gotta go, you gotta go. But for some idiotic reason known only to God, human beings create social events that resist public acknowledgement of this simple fact of nature. Case in point, the cinema. People sit for almost 2 hours consuming sodas, ice cream and assorted junk. Then everyone gets slightly pissed off when the guy in the middle row makes his way to the aisle for the bathroom. Would they prefer catheters to be handed out by the theatre owners. Or maybe the man should utilize his empty soda cup and place it under the seat when done. It would make an interesting sound effect to accompany any movie.

Another example is flatulence (a.k.a. gas, breaking wind, fart, low tide, etc.). Now nobody likes flatulence, whether it's their own or especially someone else's. But unless you like severe stomach cramps, hernias, or possible feinting spells, you're going to air out the old colon. And there is no set time or limited number for this little event. So why haven't we invented a social grace for this inevitable occurrence? It should work something like this: You're at a party, having a conversation with a group of friends. Suddenly, you feel the pressure building. You excuse yourself and walk to a part of the room where there are few or no people and announce in a moderate voice "Letting go!" You wait for a few minutes for the fumes to dissipate, then you re-join your group. This maneuver would not only acknowledge a natural bodily function as "normal" but also eliminate exposure to the dreaded S.B.D. (silent but deadly) flatulence.

- Note that in the previous paragraphs a pattern of denial exists. It seems that we (humans) have a compulsive need to deny the most inescapable of our physical/mental nature. A prime example is that as a man in his late thirties, I have yet to catch a woman in the act of breaking wind. This is a closely guarded secret rivaled only by the fail safe codes at NORAD. I figure the reason why women are sometimes temperamental is because they have to hold it in for inordinate periods of time. Now the big question is, do newlywed brides fart in front of their grooms or do they still excuse themselves to the bathroom at any given moment? To date, no married man (possibly under threat of death) has publicly answered this question.

- **Itching:** Whether we like it or not, we are creatures of the flesh, and the flesh can get irritated to a considerable degree of discomfort. A number of things can cause this, ranging from bad hygiene to allergies to wearing a particular fiber in our clothing. Now the natural solution to this problem is to scratch the irritated area. Unfortunately, only certain areas can be scratched in public without causing speculation or abandonment at group functions. Briefly detailed, they are:

a) The forehead – unless you have a bad case of acne and scratching results in popped zits, this can be interpreted as a physical display of mental activity, boredom, or stupidity (i.e. scratching your head during a difficult job interview usually means kissing that sucker goodby).

b) The neck, arms, hands, and legs – can only be scratched occasionally. Minor irritations in these areas are common. The chest, stomach and back can be included, but only on rare occasions. Frequent scratching indicates only a passing familiarity with soap and water, unless followed by a vocal excuse like, "God damn synthetics! Can't they make anything with real fibers anymore?"

Now these are the areas that you <u>NEVER SCRATCH IN PUBLIC</u> unless you are among close friends of the same sex or people who are just as uncouth and disgusting as yourself:

a) The buttocks (also known as the butt, behind, rear end, ass, and several other words too silly or disgusting to mention.): Considering what comes out of this part of your anatomy, scratching it just isn't a good idea. Period!

b) The crotch (O.K., you known all the words for men and women. Don't expect me to repeat them here): **This area is the double threat of social etiquette.** Sex and human waste! Tons of material have been written concerning society's inability to deal with sex (and the never ending saga of venereal diseases), no one is going to believe that you just have an old fashion itch in the forbidden zone that needs to be scratched (IN FRONT OF PEOPLE YET!)

c) The feet: I know, I know. You wear socks and shoes, so the surrounding temperature of the foot can surpass a summer in the Mojave Desert. And human skin has a tendency to smell and become inflamed when it sweats. So why wear shoes in a carpeted, temperature controlled building? Beats the hell out of me, unless there is a secret society that likes rancid smelling feet. Out intellectually superior society requires that we subject our feet to all type of sprays and powders in order to suppress or prevent odor and bacterial inflammation. Gee, I guess taking your shoes off at the door and cleaning the floors more than once a week is too much to ask the American populace.

**Weight gain** – I'll let you in on a little secret. The average American is Fat. The most exercise they get is when they walk to a bus or train station. Maybe a game of softball on the weekends. They eat three meals a day and occasionally snack in-between. The food is usually starchy with high caloric ingredients (little vegetables). Now, the real disturbing part of this discovery is that you must never use the "F" word in public during a general conversation. Now if the man you're talking to is a poster boy for Pillsbury, do you honestly think that upon hearing the word fat, he'll run to the nearest mirror and scream, "Oh sweet Jesus, I AM FAT! HOW? WHY ME? AAARRGHHH!"? Chances are he figured that one out when he had his toilet seat custom built.

## HONESTY

As every grade school kid knows, a very young George Washington destroyed a cherry tree on his father's land. When questioned, the kid who allegedly could not tell a lie, 'fessed up. And as we all know, little George grew up to be the first President of the U.S.A. This fable has endured history as an example of the virtues of honesty. However, history omits George Senior's response to his son, "My son, are thee so fucking stupid as to defoliate my property tree by tree?" The thump I am about to deliver to thy ass will whither in comparison to the action I shall take should this insanity occur again!" You see folks, our society encourages partial or "selective" honesty (not to be confused with lying, a distinction our political system has turned into a art form) so that we may all get along better. Here are a few examples of when and when not to be "honest":

The Interview: **Under no circumstances are you to be totally honest during a job interview.** And if you absolutely have to, be only 75% so. Why? Because the person interviewing couldn't give a damn about your integrity. They're trying to figure out if you're going to be a threat to their job or if the boss will want to get in your pants. Think not? Then why do they ask that stupid question, "How do you think people see you". Like you're really going to answer, "I give a shit?" But seriously, if you're future employer knows your honest reaction to everything, you're doomed. Then they'll honestly know how to make your life a living hell.

Parties: On the off chance that the person reading this was raised by Tibetan monks, I'll spell this one out by example: You meet an outrageously hot looking woman at a half decent party and are making good time. Just as your about to decide on the hotel, she points out a woman that resembles your least favorite uncle in drag. She says, "Doesn't that girl look nice in that dress?" You explain the uncle reference, and then she informs you that a woman is to be judged by her personality, you're just like all men, blah, blah, blah. Now the honest response would be to ask her what the hell is her problem, since you're not talking about her. But instead you'll kiss her butt and agree with anything she says in the hopes of actually kissing other parts of her anatomy later.

Parental Relations: As children, we instinctively know that lying will prevent punishment. However, children lack the creative skills to effectively lie (example: the lone 5 years old standing next to the broken vase vehemently shaking his head "no"). As teenagers, we realize that the truth can be twice as effective as a well constructed lie; "Well Uncle Phil said you and Mom drank and had sex when you were 16!" Unfortunately, the effect this type of honesty resulted in was a back hand shot across the room. The rule here is that parents can only accept total honesty when (1) you are too big to physically threatened (2) denial (in front of a close relative) would result in severe embarrassment (3) you are financially secure (4) you are supporting them (5) **all of the previous.**

The Office: Honesty only works in this situation when you are the boss or when you're saving your ass ("Not me Sir. I believe Johnson was responsible for losing that account!") When you're the boss, you can honestly tell an employee that they have paint peeling breath because, "it's for the good of office moral". A working stiff telling this to a fellow employee however, can result in a broken nose, mysteriously missing documents and furniture from your desk, or a sudden rumored popularity among the homosexual employees.

It has been noted that a sustained period of half truths and little "white lies" (a.k.a. bullshit) can lead to employees stress. This is why the ritual of the "office party" was invented. Under the guise of mild intoxication, staff members can freely confide in each other without fear of major reprisal. Just as long as the line between management and labor is not crossed, like using the senior executive's name and the phrase "simple asshole" in the same sentence.

Incidently, I've never heard of a "little black lie". Does it exist? It is better or worse than a direct lie? Can only black people use them? Just a thought.

## PUBLIC DISPLAY OF EMOTION

Everyone likes being in love, or would like to be in love. The same thing with sex, but a large part of the general population becomes annoyed at the sight of a couple doing more than holding hands. O.K., standing in the middle of a crowded sidewalk slopping over each other during rush hour is an obvious annoyance. But the real reason why people get pissed off is because they aren't getting any at the moment (or what they're getting isn't as good as what they're seeing). The same rule applies to live concerts and operas. The way I see it, if people are so damned interested in hearing the fat lady sing, they shouldn't care that Mrs. Hartford has successfully unleashed Mr. Hartford's dick from under his cummerbund during the second act.

Even verbal displays of emotion are inappropriate. If you're on a commuter train, just check out the looks of nausea on your fellow passengers' faces when the people in the middle seat say "I love you so much" in exaggerated whispers while felling-up each other. If the couple happens to resemble Ken & Barbie dolls or trolls, the negative reaction is even stronger. It's bad enough that people are reminded of the ridiculous things they say in private to their significant others. The fact that the offending couple resemble an extreme on the physical attractiveness scale is just another rap against them (i.e., good looking people think they can do whatever they want, ugly folk don't know when to quit).

## DESCRIPTIVE LANGUAGE

There is the language of the vocabulary, and then there is the vocabulary of the people. Never the twain shall meet, but sometimes they call each other on the phone. What I'm getting at is the collection of words and phrases that everyone understands even though they are not taught in school or appear in Webster's Dictionary. Only under special circumstances can they be used in public and accepted as "reasonable behavior". A few examples are:

Tit – Perfectly acceptable if you're a farmer or rancher. This also can be used at the weekly poker game, fishing/hunting trip, local strip joint, or any place where guys get together, drink beer and fart (usually in these circumstances, the plural "tits or titties" is used). When used outside these circumstances, it's considered a "crass" sexual reference or description used by a "low class" person. Oh right, like "breast" is the only word used by all men.

Dick – an interesting word in American English. It's the only word that's a nickname for a man named Richard and for the male penis, the British counter-part being "Willy". Now 'Willy' from William I can understand. But 'Dick' from Richard? From 'penis'? Somewhere in the folk lore of American history there is a truly fascinating tale of how a man named Richard became Dick (or 'a dick', as the case may be). Now, referring to someone as "a dick" is an insult (Note that once again, the public description of the sexual organ is given low, undesirable status). Yet all men think that their's is the greatest thing since scented toilet tissue. Given this schizoid situation, extreme caution is advised when using this word.

Weasel – Now here's a case of one of God's creatures getting a bad rap from man for just doing it's job. Looking like a cross between a cat and a mouse, this animal eats small birds and eggs as part of it's diet. So when European farmers showed up on the Great Frontier with domesticated chickens, the weasel community said "Party On!!" A generation later, the weasel still manages to make a fool of the American farmer; by-passing guard dogs, electric fences, traps and locked doors. So naturally, it's considered the scum of the earth because it can't be trusted to do the right thing and starve to death while man takes all the natural resources for himself. This is why the word "weasel" has come to be the equivalent of calling someone an untrustworthy or a thief. My question is why hasn't "weasel" been substituted for the word "businessman"?

Ho – a classic example of slang Americana! Repeated three times, it's the trademark laugh of a mythical fat man that delivers toys on December 25th. Add the letter 'E' on the end, and you've named a garden tool. But DO NOT use it in the same sentence when describing some guy's wife, girlfriend, mother, or any female relative. In this context, you're saying the woman is a member of the world's oldest profession (THEM'S FIGHT'IN WORDS, PARDNER). Which might explain why Santa was always so damn jolly. Ho, HO, HO!!

## CLOTHING STYLE

Perhaps one of the most intricate and somewhat bizarre aspects of social standing. Time was when your clothing told people exactly what you were (doing) in life. Jeans and T-shirt meant blue collar worker, jacket and tie meant office worker, three piece suit meant executive/businessman. Now-a-days, the grubby looking schmoe with torn jeans standing next to Mr. $500 suit probably owns a courier service and is worth several hundred grand. Meanwhile, Mr. Fashion Plate is sweating out the morning stock report, given that at any moment he'll be worth a train ticket and how much he can pawn his CD sound system for. My point is that clothes don't always "make the man". Prime examples are:

1) Form fitting clothes: Please, please, PLEASE do not wear these unless you have a form worth fitting. Nothing puts off the potential dates more than a flabby person trying to squeeze their butt into a pair of Guess jeans or pretend their gut isn't spilling over in a tight mock turtle neck shirt. Once again, financial status can excuse this problem (yes, we are a shallow breed), but don't bet the farm on it.

2) Over dressing: Showing up in a dress or shirt & tie at a barbecue indicates snobbishness or geekdom (Wealth does not excuse geekdom). A good excuse is that all your regular stuff is in the wash. Note that if you happen to look like a centerfold (Playboy or Playgirl), no one will give a damn what you wear. Just as long as its tight.

## COMMON OBSERVATIONS NEVER STATED IN PUBLIC

- No one will ever admit the real reason why they hate "The Ballet". Look, when a swan dies, it just keels over and drifts until some alligator scarfs it down. It does not dance on the water from one gay swan to another, doing pirouettes and waving its wings to symphony music.

- Interesting how people with a vicious influenza will go out to party, indifferent as to how many innocent victims they infect; but if they have a small juice stain on their "attire" you would need a cattle prod to get them out the door on time. Ah, priorities.

-    In the recent years it seems that some small whales have become suicidal and try to beach themselves, predominantly on the California coast.  You never see a giant Sperm whale suddenly saying, "AWW Fuck it!" and throwing itself up on Coney Island, do you?  Then you have all these environmental people running down to the beach and spending hours dragging these little (1/2 a ton little) manic depressants back into the sea, only to have half the number back on the sand an hour later.  What the TV cameras and newspaper don't cover are the exhausted humanitarians cursing and kicking a beached whale whom they realized they saved not more than 3 hours ago.  It's like a shrink giving a long term patient a clean bill of health, only to have him zip by his 8th floor office window 15 minutes later.  Frustrating, to say the least.

-    The look of sheer horror that comes over a man's face when he realizes his barber has an erection when shaving him!

-    Women who complain they are rarely sexually satisfied are the ones that kiss their dogs on the lips.  THEN they kiss their boyfriends.

-    The inability of people to tell a co-worker that their deodorant is (literally) not up to snuff that day.  Most suffer in silence, because telling the truth in such cases is an insult to be remembered for life.  Why?  If I'm about to attract flies or make people frown without uttering a word, I sure as hell would want someone tell me!  Now if these people are oblivious to their funky fragrance, a casual comment can be most effective; "You know Mary, I saw a doctor on TV that said daily bathing in conjunction with anti-perspirants and such prevent most smells during the work day.  It's **amazing** how many **people forget that,** don't **you** think?"

-    It stands to reason that all public transportation systems should install special seats for fat people.  I'm talking big, the people that breath heavy just from picking up a newspaper.  Now most buses and commuter trains have 3 seats to a row.  If some fat ass unfolds in the middle, no one else can sit down.  If they take the window seat, only one person can get the aisle seat.  And if they're in the aisle seat, it's like crossing the Alps to get to the window.  To avoid all this, just have a few special rows set up for these folks.  The only modification would be that a 3 seat row would be two seats, with one cheek separator removed.  And a small sign saying, "250 lbs. and up".

-    Evidently, common courtesy is based on mutual economic status.  Just witness a well dressed, well groomed person trip and almost fall on the payment in the business district.  At least 3 or 4 people will stop, help that person, and make sure they're alright.  Now at the same time, the homeless man whose been on that street for 5 years coughs violently and decomposes into a steaming pile of rags and human remains.  Not only will passers-by try and ignore the scene but someone is sure to comment, "Look at that.  Guy turns to shit and City Sanitation leaves him there.  What the hell are we paying taxes for?"

-    Will someone please explain why "women's" magazines like Cosmopolitan have their cover girls dress like sex toys?  Now the average American woman does not have a model's figure with C-cup cleavage.  If they did you wouldn't have all those damned info-mercials pushing butt crunchers and slim fast.  Therefore, this type of "wish fulfillment" advertising should piss off most women and turn on most men.  But since the magazine is not geared towards men (and men don't buy it, just gawk at the covers), I can only suspect a hidden lesbian agenda here.

-       Every now and then the local press will cover some rich person throwing a big event to raise money for some favorite charity.  Great detail is given to the viewpoints of the attending politicians, businessmen and celebrities.  However, no one bothers to compare the <u>actual cost</u> of this event <u>against</u> the amount raised by these society bigwigs.  If they did, I bet it would be the equivalent of buying a tux and limousine in order to drop $5 bucks in the cup of the squeegee man at the Lincoln Tunnel.

-       People will go their entire lives associating with those they cannot stand!  This is done in the name of 'manners and politeness'.  You never hear someone say, "I can't take the sight of you Phil.  Let's have lunch!"  Instead, Phil thinks he's made a great acquaintance, while his host secretly complains to relatives and friends of "having to put up with that asshole".  This ritual is done for the following reasons; (1) pay off- there is something to be gained by appeasing people who annoy you (examples: your boss, rich-in-law, the geek with the well built, nymphomaniac sister).  (2) coercion – your mother, wife, husband, father, kids, boss, or anyone who has some kind of hold over you makes you do it.

Note that the animal kingdom has this particular problem licked.  The male lion, for instance, gets horny, stakes out several females (via fist fights) and sires a slew of kids.  Nobody comes or go's unless he says so.  Then he gets bored and leaves.  At the same time, the female lion raises the kids to a certain age, slaps them in the head to get out and on their own.  She then books, looking to hook up with another harem.  Hey, it ain't Disney's "The Lion King" and yes, it is barbaric and sexist by human standards.  But you'll never hear this argument among a lion family, "Aww shit honey.  Do we have to have the Brown's over again this month!?!"  'If I have to put up with your damn poker buddies we do!'

## INITIATIVE IN THE WORK PLACE

In a country that historically admires the rugged individual that "pioneered" this or "developed a new" that, notice how hard it is to get people to volunteer.  That's because most volunteers end up doing what is commonly known as "the shit work".  Now the person that volunteers on his own without being asked is usually touted by his boss as "showing initiative".  On the other hand, fellow employees know this person as a "kiss ass" and other colorful characterizations.  It is a thin line to walk, and here a few helpful pointers:

<u>Food</u>:  If you suggest "everyone bring something" to the office Christmas party, you jolly well better be the best fucking cook in the State.  And cook a WHOLE LOTTA STUFF.  That way, you avoid the suck-up of the year label for talking the boss out of catering a free meal for the staff.  And no one will feel guilty for emptying a box of Chips Ahoy on a dish and calling it "an old family recipe".

<u>Overtime</u>:  Now everyone likes a little extra in the ol' paycheck.  So getting a jump on tomorrow's work pile is acceptable.  It starts getting risky when you decide to "take the initiative" and start doing stuff that's not necessary (like cross referencing the boss's files with yours).  Nothing burns the ass of a fellow employee more than to be compared to "that go-getter who puts his overtime to good use".  Note that these go-getters seldom get invited to parties and have a high incidence of unexplained scratches on their cars.

<u>Input</u>:  Right, so you're smarter than everyone else at the staff meeting.  You just have all the God damned answers.  But if you were <u>really</u> smart, you'd keep your mouth shut and let the other wage slaves come up with some something.  Why?  Because then you'll be seen as a savior when the boss asks several questions and the response is dead silence.

## THE BATTLE OF THE SEXES

Now there is a "battle of the sexes" constantly being waged in the good old U.S. of A. Some people are trying to make peace, but as always Americans tend to over-do things. I question anyone who tells me to get in touch with my "feminine side" (incidently, is that the left or right side?) I mean, the Pope recently declared that touching my male side is a sin! But, I digress; each side has major complaints about the other that are seldom made public (except by some shrink out for a fast buck, or by caring, sincere people like myself). So here are a few secret complaints that should help you understand the opposite sex better (or dump the clown your currently dating):

### Insincerity

- Women will dump a man faster than yesterday's garbage the second they discover he was always more interested physically than emotionally. He has done her wrong. Yet, in less then 24 hours she's engaged to Mr. Right, a co-worker whom she "always hoped would notice her". Did it ever occur to her that a definition of insincere could be using a guy as a sexual bus stop while she's waiting to ride a Greyhound?

- Now by the same token, most men are perfectly comfortable with jumping on anything in a skirt right up to 2 weeks before getting married. But the wedding's off if he suspects she's even thinking about an ex-flame. After all, he's getting rid of all impure thoughts of other women prior to the wedding. The fact that doing it physically annoys the fiance somehow escapes him.

- Only in recent years has the subject of "faking it" has been discussed publicly via social psychology literature, TV talk show hosts, and any fool that can get 5 minutes of air time on a local radio station. Now the story thus far is that when a woman isn't always sexually satisfied by her partner, and she occasionally fakes orgasm (completely fooling the man.) This is done so the man's self-confidence won't be destroyed, etc. etc. Now instead of deception, why doesn't the woman just wait until he leaves, then change her door lock and phone number (if married, withdrawal from the joint account and relocation without a forwarding address is advised). This avoids those messy confessions and having to endure the time honored retort, "OH Yeah, maybe it's you?"

Men, on the other hand, can never actually "fake it" in the traditional sense (a cruel trick of nature). We go the more cerebral route, using imagination. Problem is that sometimes our vocal cords don't always catch up with our cognitive reasoning skills. This usually results in screaming "Oh Jane baby!" at the crucial moment when the partner at hand is named Ethel. Following this mistake, we complete the mental exercise of faking by saying "Of course I love you!" This action is also known by it's common name, lying.

### Attraction or "what gives?"

- From the time we are born, we are subjected to images of what the ideal man or woman should look like. Television, movies, magazines, family and friends all reinforce these images. However, in real life all men do not look like Tarzan and all women do not look like a Playboy bunny. Which is a shame, because the debate on attractiveness is the core of the battle of the sexes. Now few people in either camp will admit that they would partner with the aforementioned stereotype (or a reasonable facsimile) in a heartbeat, for fear of being called "shallow". So as I see it, there is a massive secret society of shallow people that buy all the skin mags, promote all the movie idols, endorse all the model advertisement, and pay all the plastic surgeons.

- In my lifetime I have always heard women say that they are different from men in that they are more attracted to the man's personality than his physical looks. This suggest that we men are bio-mechanical dolts that will cozy up to an axe murderer as long as she looks good. This is fascinating, because women must be able to perform a Vulcan Mind Meld from a distance before they can get turned on. Now that's science fiction ladies. Science fact is that in America there are 5 women to every 1 man. So the next time you see some stunning woman on the arm of a missing link, chances are it's "slim pick'ins" at work rather than superior emotional bonding.

- Have you ever notices that the majority of plastic surgeons look like prime candidates for their own techniques? Hint: If these people are doing stuff to you that they won't (but can afford to) have done to themselves, something's up.

- In the battle of the sexes, the American male has time and time again demonstrated his ability to shoot himself in the foot. Case in point, the time honored debate over penile size determining sexual attractiveness. The origin of this argument started when some pre-historic simpleton, jealous of a friends popularity with the cave girls, noticed that his friends dick dwarfed his own by comparison. Thus began the unwritten law that "women like big ones". Somehow, women got wind of this attitude and have used it to their advantage ever since. To date, get ten women together, and they'll debate till dawn over what size and shape is generally preferred. So guys, rest assured that if your partner says what you've got is "enough for her", believe her. However, if you find a copy of PlayGirl under the bed with the photo spread of "Johnny Wad" severely dog-eared, you might want to take a trip to the old plastic surgeon. Or therapist. Or both!

## JEALOUSY

Show me just <u>one</u> person who has <u>never</u> been jealous of their spouse, girl or boyfriend and I'll show you an alien disguised as a human being. Either that or a person destined for sainthood. Jealousy, whether we like it or not, does become the human animal. And in case you're one of those people who say "Not Me!", here are a three classic examples I'm sure you'll recognize:

<u>Improves senses</u> – before the love of your life, your powers of observation were pretty normal. But the second your significant other pays slight attention to someone of the opposite sex (other than you), you become the reincarnation of Sherlock Holmes. Guys will deduce that their girlfriend has the hots for Mr. GQ sitting across from their restaurant table by the way a vein in the neck pulses quicker whenever her eyes stray in that direction. Girls will swear that their man has cheating on his mind because he doesn't breath the same old way when she holds his hand.

<u>Enhanced memory</u> – You forget where you place the car keys every morning; constantly forget co-workers' names, parents, birthdays, and wash day for underwear. Yet while watching TV, your loved one says, "I don't see what's so attractive about him/her?", you vividly remember 6 years ago during a pool party where they drooled over a person just like the one on TV. You know this because it was at 7:45 p.m., a pleasant 78 degrees; 40 party guests, half of them married couples; the host was wearing Birkenstock sandals, the hostess served canapes with white wine when your partner asked, **"Who's that** on the diving board"?

Regression – Remember during childhood, you had a toy that was hardly ever played with. Yet if some other kid picked it up, you charged over screaming "MINE!" and held on to it for dear life. Now as an adult, you go to some affair and abandon your partner because they're with a group of friends (of the same sex). But the second, you see them enjoying the company of someone of the opposite sex, you two become joined at the hip for the rest of the evening (which becomes embarrassing when trying to go to the bathroom). I guess old habits die hard.

Another example of childishness resulting from jealousy is demanding to be the center of your partners attention in a group situation. Now if you don't get it you do the adult equivalent of pouting and whining; standing alone in kitchen and answering every question with "Nothings wrong, I just want to be by myself".

## Forbidden Questions

… Why do we say stupid things like "The anniversary of Pearl Harbor" or "The anniversary of the Death of (fill in celebrity of choice)? If only anniversary weren't such a happy sounding word. I mean, did you ever see people partying in the streets over death and destruction?

… If masturbation is a sin as declared by Pope John Paul II, then just how do priests and nuns control "the urge" if they've taken a vow of celibacy? I'll wager if you enter them in the Olympic shot put, pole and wrestling divisions, the U.S.A. would make a clean sweep. Also, the Vatican must have a laundry bill a third size of the national deficit.

…For all Frankenstein, Dracula, and Werewolf movies: Why don't the villagers **just move out** instead of hanging around and letting the monster beat the shit out of them on a regular basis? Probably they're afraid of being labeled "fucking stupid" by other villages for taking so long to do so.

# Random Thoughts
by Vincent Jenkins

If any of this seems slightly cynical to you, guess what?  IT IS!

<u>Pets</u>

-    A lot of scary stuff going on with science now-a-days.  They're seriously into gene splicing, cloning, all the Star Trek stuff which can have a lot of benefits in our every day lives.  Like those shopping ladies that bop around 5th avenue can soon have a little dog that's perfect for carrying around in those damn handbags of theirs.  It'll have no legs, tail or butt, just a head and a tube like body that only needs water and sunlight to live.  They'll come in plaid, autumn brown, or some perfect accessory color for the smart dressed woman.

-    You'll no longer have to destroy your cat's identity and self esteem by having it "fixed" (such a calming, misleading word) and then take away it's only means of self defense by having it "de-clawed".  In a few years, cats will be fuzzy, round little nerf like things.  You can bounce'em off walls and stuff.  Stick'em to velcro when you leave the apartment.

-    Yes, Pet Owning.  The art of surgically mutilating trusting dumb animals to become live in toys for the average family.  Ever notice how people will talk about their "pet canary" or "pet monkey", as oppose to the canary and monkey that's just hanging around the house.  "Well these two belong to me and wife, the other monkey just stopped by to tape Wild Kingdom on the VCR".

-    What kills me is when you bust chops on a pet owner.  They get that fierce somewhat glazed look in their eyes and state the Pet Owner credo; "You must have your pet spayed or neutered for it's own good."  Oh, I understand.  You breed dogs and cats for the express purpose of separating them from their own kind and selling them to people who raise it almost exclusively around humans, crippling it's instinct to survive in the wild.  And then you destroy it's sexual identity.  My theory is you give the potential owners an instruction manual and a surgical kit with each pet purchase, and you see how fast pet shops would close around town.  "OK Mrs. Johnson, that'll be $200 for the puppy and $187 for the spaying kit.  Now I can throw in the smock and rubber gloves for an additional $10.  Believe me, first time can sometimes be, aahh, a little messy.  But if you blow it, just bring the little fellah right in for an estimate, and my cousin Paulie the Vet will see what he can do."

-    Look, I like cats, dogs, etc.  I <u>don't like</u> pet owners who treat them like people.  You know the ones that have a thousand stories of Kitty doing this or Spanky doing that, how they have "human like" responses, etc., etc.  You know damn well if Kitty pulled a Mister Ed and actually asked for a sandwich, the owner would either have a massive coronary or Kitty's ass would be waffled into the floor with an available blunt instrument.  Most likely the owner would be straight jacketed, screaming, "BUT HE TALKED, HE TALKED!" all the way to Bellevue.

-    And what is this nonsense with pet reptiles?  Someone please explain to me what pleasure can be derived from watching something with no discernable expression of emotion sitting absolutely still for hours?  Or what's so entertaining about watching bugs and small rodents being eaten live?  Ever see snakes or lizards wag their tails when the owner comes home?  They don't give a good God damn who you are, just as long as the food keeps coming.  The owners are obviously people with an incredibly low entertainment threshold; "Oh, look. Muffy's slithering across the floor! Now she's stopping, now she's wrapping herself around the garbage can! Isn't that cute?!" At least with a fish tank you get a live TV of sorts.

- Another bizarre trait of pet owners is their habit of subjecting unsuspecting guest to their pets particular instinctive traits. Example, the bird owner. They'll tell a guest that they can let the Brazilian parrot walk on them because he's "friendly". What they don't tell the guest is that a parrot's beak has the ability to crack walnut shells, and that he instinctively uses his beak to "test" the foundation of anything he's about to climb on. Also, parrots instinctively perch at the highest level available for security. So the owners shouldn't be too surprised when they return from the kitchen and find their guest writhing on floor with several bloody dents running from their hand to their shoulder, bird shit on their heads, and feathery lump of something piled next to them.

## Computers

- I love it when the science community announces a revolutionary breakthrough in computer software technology for business that will increase production speed, etc., etc. They forget to mention that as a direct result of this break through, most likely your job won't be necessary anymore.

- Another scary thing is this virtual reality stuff. Kids slip on goggles and gloves and they see only a computer graphic world where they can move stuff around. Pretty soon they'll have a holographic room where you create your own world. Sight, smell, touch, the works. Picture this, a tropical beach setting, warm breeze, moonlight. You've just had the BEST SEX OF YOUR LIFE WITH THE FANTASY PARTNER OF YOUR DREAMS. Laying in the after glow, you feel so damn good, you ask confidently "Now wasn't that great baby?" And your partner smile and says, "SEGA!!"

## Cosmetics

- And of course, we can't discuss medical advancement without getting into COSMETIC SURGERY. Now just for the record, it's your money, it's your body, do whatever the hell you want. Just be realistic. I mean, chances are if you're a man, a hair transplant is not going to make you more attractive on the beach if you've still got a hairy beer belly hanging over those French bikini briefs! And ladies, if you can't see your feet anymore, you've just gone to far.

- Now they've finally got that long awaited surgical procedure for men. For those of who have eaten, I'll be brief. The surgeon CUTS into the ligaments along side the shaft, the guys penis accordion's out an inch or two. If it looks silly, they take some fat out of your butt and pad it out to proportion. Patch you up, and send you home the same day. My question is, save for a very surprised girlfriend and/or wife, Who's going to know the difference?!?! I mean if a woman gets breast implants, everyone sees the results. How does a guy advertise! Custom made pants? Work it into a conversation at the office or a party? "Yeah, Wall Street kicked my ass so bad last month, I had to extend the car loan. But ya know, for $2 grand I got a 1 inch extension on my dick. Good deal, man. Good deal!"

- Or maybe just spring it on the boys in the shower room after the weekly basketball game: "Man, we'll kick some ass in the playoffs next week! Yo, Frank pass me the towel... WHOA, WHAT THE HELL IS THAT?!? WHAT THE FUCK HAPPENED TO YOU!!? Hey! Ya'll check this out! Umph, Umph, Umph! Boy done lost his mind."

---------------------------

- Just goes to show you the lengths to which people will go in the name of "good looks". Craziest thing I ever seen are those Info-mercials? You know, the hour long commercials for selling products that explain themselves on the side of the container (read in less than 3 minutes), with some clown on the verge of hysteria prompting a paid audience? And sometimes, if you're real lucky, there'll be some known actor (trying to make a down payment on his new house) whose JUST CRAZY about this product.

- I saw one for Ron Popiel's Instant Hair. Yep, the man that gave you the Pocket Fisherman, the Veg-a-matic, Mr. Microphone, and all those wonderfully cheap plastic devices over the years is now qualified to sell Hair in a can for people who are losing theirs but hate toupee's. Classic suspension of belief to buy this one. There's ol' Ron Popiel standing over some middle aged simp with a serious Friar Truck bald spot, spraying stuff all over the place while frantically combing what few strands of hair Nature and God have left the man. After a few minutes, we come back and, Why, Friar Tuck is amazed at how good his head looks. "My God Ron, I wouldn't have believed I could have hair like this again!!"

- Does anyone remember G.I. Joe action doll with life like hair? If your wondering what they did with all those doll heads, just watch this nonsense and then tell me different! Pretty soon we'll see Ron Popiel and the President of Hasbro toys in front of Judge Wopner on Channel 5. How in the world can these people make you believe this stuff when your watching TV and you can SEE a man with plastic dust covering a bald spot on his head? What really scared me was when Ron Popiel assures us that this product is non-toxic, non-flammable and can wash out in a few hours. Good to know, since your head could be near an open flame at any moment. Like people are going to spray this on before they go out and say, "Whoops, better put a match to my head and check this stuff out!" "Better spray some around the pet canary and see if it's still standing while I back the car out."

## Job Market

- Have you been unemployed? Collect unemployment insurance? What test do you have to fail to work for the Unemployment Insurance section of the State Labor Dept.? I've always imagine that some of the qualifications on the job description read like: Must have a little or no patience:, Total disregard for fellow human beings; Must be able to ask totally ridiculous or painfully obvious questions; Must be able to identify crucial information pertaining to client, and lose said information.

- The State finally got smart a few years back. Rather than risk contributing to the country's homicide rate on a daily basis, they started using computers. That way, there's no on person to blame for depriving you of half the money you should be getting from all that stuff they took out of your check when you were working. God Bless America.

- And the employment agencies are no better. Whether it's the fancy Park Avenue office or some closet in the Village, they tell more lies than a 17 year old prom queen who comes home at 3 a.m. with her dress on backwards! I don't care what the advertisement says in the New York Times "Help Wanted" section, if you can't type 55 wpm or better, start memorizing the breakfast list at McDonald's. It's like they're searching for that one person who'll have a nervous breakdown if pushed. No Lie. While sweating out an interview once, I saw a middle aged guy right out of a Norman Rockwell painting walk into the agency and tell the receptionist he was answering the ad for a senior middle management position at a top N.Y architecture firm. The receptionist, and obvious graduate of the John Gotti secretarial school says, "Showah hon, fill this out and we'll have yuse do a typing test."

Then to add insult to injury, the clown (or consultant as they like to be called) that ran the ad bounces out of the back room states the Personnel Agency Standard Lie, "The client is making a decision on some earlier applicants and there's nothing else in your salary range right now. Let's try some alternatives." I thought I was finally going to see justice in the form of these morons getting bitch-slapped into next Tuesday. And he did just what the rest of us would have done, wimped out and left his resume.


Sex/Men and Women

-    So the Surgeon General gets fired for off handedly suggesting that masturbation be part of the sex education curriculum in our public schools. OH NO, THE BIG 'M'! THE JERKING OF THE EVIL HAND! THE FOOLISH FINGERING OF FATE! THE END OF THE WORLD! **Give me a goddamn break!** What's left? Good old fashion sex isn't possible unless you wrap yourself in plastic or wait six months worth of blood test. All the big popular religions say no sex until your past 17 and married. Except the Episcopalians, who allow "monogamous non-married" relations (just to piss off the Catholics).

So you get acquainted, a little heavy petting, meet the parents, get the blood test, spend the money, get married, then find out he or she is lousy in bed. Why? They didn't practice! And the Pope says the masturbation is a sin! So no matter what good deeds you do in life, when you die you've got to pull a little time in Hell for all that quality time spent in bathroom during your teens.

-    The singles bar scene is out because you might fall in love with a Trans-something or other from the Sally-Orphan-Phil-Geraldo show. There's the on-going battle by special interest groups to ban sex magazines, adult theaters, sex novelty shops, suggestive television. So what the hell is left. If I hear one more time, "If you truly believe in love and God, you'll wait for that special someone in marriage" **I WILL COMMIT MURDER.** If everyone thought that way, the psychologist couldn't meet the demands. Scores of young people lined up some poor Ph.D.'s office:

(Big sigh), so Mr. Williams, you say that these, ah, 'wet dreams' have not only increased in intensity but frequency as well?"

(Near Hysterical) They don't even wait until I'm sleep Doc. All I gotta do is daydream during a boring day at work and it's another pair of Geoffrey Beenes shot to hell. I had to start wear'in Depends, and I'm only 19! Help me Doctor!!!

Yes, Well, were out of time. Let's increase your valium and pick this up next week. Nurse, send in Number 27.

-    Despite all of this, the battle of the sexes rages on. Men and women continue the one upmanship in a relation, trying to look like their in control in front of their friends. The major weapon women have in this time honored silliness is the annoying ability to change their minds. And the man's weapon is to resort to the simply childish yet effective method of walking away.

Example, I had a pet name for my ex-girlfriend that I won't nauseate you with. Anyway, one day she reads me the riot act "I wish you would stop calling me that stupid name. I am not a child, I am not your child or pet or toy. Cut it out!"

So I didn't see her for two weeks, then on Valentines day, at a not too shabby restaurant I gave her a card. She rips it open, scans every corner like there was hidden money in it, looks at me and says (trembling, sad, child like voice) "You didn't use my pet name. YOU DON'T LOVE ME ANYMORE!" Bolts from the table for the bathroom. Now you can't in any way retaliate because you know everyone in the restaurant within earshot has you tagged as an unfeeling bastard who's obviously trifled with the poor woman's affection. At least that's what all the women were loudly whispering to their men. And the men won't even look in your direction for fear that somehow, it will be interpreted as sympathy, resulting in no future dinner and/or sex. So I did what any honorable man could do, left without paying the check while she was still in the bathroom. Bastard they wanted, bastard they got.

-    Then there's the constant game of Ready or Not. You're ready, she's not and vice versa. There's not a man alive who has not heard this from his wife or girlfriend, "SEX! SEX! SEX! I swear, that's all you have on your mind!". But, the **ONE TIME** you're not in the mood, she's like a Bengal Tiger in heat. You can be driving on the highway looking for an off ramp, doing 65 m.p.h, and she gets that look in her eye. Starts playing with your shirt sleeve and stuff. And it's Judgement Day and Armageddon if you say no.

"Well I'M SORRY if I'm bothering you! I remember a time when you couldn't keep your hands off of me!"

"Yeah, but usually I didn't have to worry about being impaled by a fuck'in steering wheel, did I?!!"

-    There are problems between the sexes because the unspoken Puritanical ethic that rules every aspect of this country causes confusion at young ages. Think not? Remember that asinine kids cartoon that was shoved down your throat during the eighties? The Smurfs? I watched that with my kid nephews. There was Old Papa Smurf, 1 Baby Smurf, 1 Smurfette (female), and a slew of assorted male Smurfs in their early twenties. But Baby Smurf had no father or mother, he was **just there.** At least one of the male Smurfs would try and date Smurfette, and usually fail. Papa Smurf had **no wife and none was ever mentioned!** Now, were the fuck did they all come from? Are they all related to each other? None of 'em even laid eggs!! Hell, after being brainwashed with this crap, I would be relieved to catch my youngster beating off in the bathroom with a copy of Playboy. At least you know he's on the right track!

-    Points of contention in the male/female relationship: Women will not date a man because "he's immature", these "mature" women keep a Teddy Bear named Mr. Snuggles on their pillow; Men complain that they girlfriends "don't give me enough space", yet are pissed off when they call at some bizarre hour and her message machine says she's out having fun with her girlfriends or family, **without him.**

-    For the record: Women who say "Yuck, body builders!" and men who say "Playboy bunnies, not really my type!" **are both lying through their teeth**. Notice that their heads swivel with a reaction time that would put Pavlov's dog to shame every time one of these body types are in range. It's like an old time Mormon saying sex and 15 year old girls never occupy his mind at the same time.

-      When it comes to divorce, you really can't blame either man or woman.  Let's get real!  Memories of that beautiful, frisky, perfect person you dated go right out the window every morning when faced with the reality of a bleary eyed, farting creature with dragon breath who demands you get out of the bathroom 5 minutes early.

## Observations

-      I don't know why everyone panics over the new right wing tilt on the Supreme Court.  With all the indications of the new Congress and Senate, one day soon Judges Clarence Thomas, Sandra Day O'Conner and Anton Scalia will be heading for chambers, only to find the door closed with a sign nailed on reading WEALTHY WHITE ANGLO SAXON PROTESTANT MALES ONLY.  If the Democrats can't get anyone in after that, the hell with'em.  Could you imagine Clarence Thomas's reaction?  "What the?!?!  Those Mutha Fucka's.  So that's what I was signing last week.  Sheeit!"

-      Isn't it great how every new government administration claims that unemployment is down, etc., etc.  You read this in your morning papers as you avoid the guys who have been asking for spare change for the past ten years.

-      For the record:  Richard Nixon and his advisors nearly subvert the entire free electoral process and Congressional mandate, orders a secret war in Vietnam: he's revered for his smart foreign policy and all but sanctified upon his death; Oliver North commits the treasonable act of dealing drugs and weapons with registered enemies of the America: he gets off and later runs for Congress; George Bush's son was a major player in the S&L scandal which nearly bankrupts the nation: he gets elected to Congress; You and I are late with ONE $60 credit card payment, are labeled as a credit risk, charged outrages interest rates, are threatened by collection agencies and have our financial and social future placed in jeopardy.  Yep, that sounds fair.

-      If the FCC goes to great lengths to have commercials be as truthful as possible, then why can't toilet tissue commercials demonstrate the product in actual use?  Let's have Mr. Bradley being secretly taped using Brand X and the new improved whatever in the Men's room at Penn Station.  In fact why don't they use this type of "test" for all service oriented commercials: *What the plaintive Mr. Cannon doesn't know is that we've secretly switched his family's attorney with our new "Philip & Marlowe Law Firm" attorney.  Let's watch…*

-      Why is it that most credit card commercials rarely mention that you're going to have TO PAY for all that wonderful stuff IN LESS THAN 1 MONTH FROM THE INITIAL CHARGED?

-      Don't you love watching snotty uptown yuppies putting their Wall Street manicured hands into a baggie and picking up their dog's shift?  Tops off my day.

-      For the New York region, the commercial that gets the **"It' a Goddamn Lie!"** award goes to the Long Island Rail Road.  The one were a voice-over states how he helps his passengers "make the transition a little easier" to and from the hectic work day in New York City.  The T.V. shows a smiling conductor walking the clean, sun lit aisles saying hello to regulars who sit comfortably spaced apart, taking tickets.

I take the L.I.R.R., this is how it goes:  You've had a lousy day at work.  You rush down to Penn Station, shove through crowds, dive onto an either too hot or cold crowded car, sit in a seat sandwiched between two truly obese people with bad breath and gas who loudly and continuously remark on how ridiculously crowded it is.  Then as you finally ignore the aroma coming from the toilet at the opposite end of the car, find some comfort and close your eyes for that 2 hour ride, some graying, pony tailed, pot bellied ex-hippie in a 1940's hotel page boy uniform, brays out ALL TICKETS PLEASE.  The fat bookends start pocket digging for their tickets, giving you a nice rib massage, and the train starts demonstrating that it needs new shocks.  Yeah, having a bad middle aged impersonation of Ringo Starr taking my tickets makes it all just a little bit better.

-    Funny how in a large, crowded restaurant some people will bitch and moan, go into convulsions because one smoker in the men's room on the opposite end of the place.  But no one will admit to their eyes tearing from the over-powering fog of "Drakkar" that some guy bathed himself in.  Obviously no one has explained the difference between "pleasant fragrance" and "oxygen depletion" to him.

-    God love Animal fur activist:  Throwing paint on expensive furs while zipping up their all natural 3% wool, jackets against the cold.  Marching stoically up and down Fifth Avenue screaming for the humane rights of Chinchillas as they step over homeless people.  And after littering the streets with their flyers, they take the train to the suburbs to sit down to a chicken dinner.  Am I missing something here?

-    People wonder why today's youth are so confused.  Here's a possibility: for the first 3 years of it's life, a baby is confronted by these huge beings who speak gibberish to them in weird tones, are constantly being poked in the stomach and carried around like a football.  And you wonder why babies pass their body weight in shit every 3 hours!

-    If nuclear power is so safe, why do the major congressional and business supporters have residence in the cities that <u>don't</u> have power plants?

-    The female members of a suburban type community will protest topless bars near their neighborhood.  Yet check out the mail boxes in the same neighborhood and count the subscriptions to "Victoria's Secrets Catalogue" by the same women.  You don't need Freud for this one.


<u>The Great Race</u>

-    During my grandparents time, we were Colored People, then Negroes.  During my Parents time we were Negroes, then Afro-Americans, then Blacks.  During my time we were Afro-Americans, then Blacks, and currently are African-Americans.  In another generation, we'll be like Prince the musician, just a symbol with a phonetic sound like UGH!!

-    There will be peace in America just as soon as everyone can trace his or her ethnic and racial roots right back to the Jurassic Period.  People just have to know every stick in that woodpile.  Why not capitalize on this:

> Yes, welcome to Spot the Negro.  Our contestant of the day is Mrs. Jane Dakota from Butte, Montana.  Now for the final grand prize of $5,000.00 Mrs. Dakota, which one of our three panelist is really a Negro.  Is it #1 accountant Mr. Roger Siskel, #2 screenwriter Albert Ventura, or #3 teacher Clifton Samuels.
> #Gee, it's so confusing, there all so swarthy looking.  But I'll have to go with #3*<

> Oh I'm sorry Mrs. Dakota. It's not #3. In fact, all of our panelist are technically Caucasian. The real Negro is in fact your husband Arvil, on his Mother's side of the family!<

- Why is the rest of America still freaked out when a person of Oriental heritage speaks with a regional accent? Maybe the guy has a "Bawhstun" accent because his family has been there since 1850! What the hell do you want, a dubbed voice from a Godzilla movie? I can't even understand the kids in my neighborhood with "YO YO Bees UP Ya'll?", and people are bothered because the man doesn't sound like Charlie Chan?

- Yep, audio-racial identification. I always run into a similar problem, but I've learned to have fun with it. When I was job hunting on Long Island straight out of college, I would give great phone interviews, practically be promised the job. Then I would show up at the interview. I just can't resist watching people get that frozen smile on their faces while they break out in a cold sweat!

"Good afternoon, we spoke on the telephone earlier today. I am Mr. Jenkins. I'm here for the administrative assistant interview". The secretary would smile, ask me to have a seat as she went to announce me.

(muffled, excitable female voice) Mr. Smith, there's a big Negro in the outer office. He's your 3:30!

(astonished, hushed upper class male voice) What! I thought you said this man sounded OK on the phone, Ms. Jones?

(rising panic) WELL HE DID TOO! Maybe he was raised by missionaries or something?

At this point, just to really get things going, I'd knock on the office door. "Excuse me, Ms. Jones? Could I use your phone to call my cousin? He a lawyer for the ACLU, and I told him I would buy lunch today, depending upon the outcome of today's interview."

- Of all the racial sterio-types in the world, the one that really gets me is the sterio-type of Swedish people. You know, "they're all built like gods, have the sexual drive of rabbits, and are outrageously creative in bed, etc., etc.". Why, what a horrible, derogatory thing to say! Face it, someone calling you, "… a fantastic, sexy pagan god" isn't exactly going to piss you off.

- You know something is up when the best soul music you hear on the radio is a white band from England, and one of the top jazz groups touring the U.S. is Japanese.


Clothing & Styles

- Use to be when a black kid was wearing jeans that couldn't get over his butt, they were European cut. Now they're what, $50.00?

- The Grunge look. There's something to be said for a culture where people spend good money to buy clothes that make them look dirt poor. "Idiotic" comes to mind.

- Every year, rich people gather in France to see the latest fashion creations by designers who themselves either resemble trolls or are just plain weird. And these folks determine what you and I wear. Why are these people paid millions to design clothes that I recognize in photos of my great grand father? Since when did we go from bell bottoms and 3 inch heel shoes back to suspenders, oxfords and bow ties? Looks more like the school of design plagiarism to me.

- A typical New Yorker can be arrested as a suspected terrorist stepping off a plane anywhere in the world. Why? Our hip dress style of a black jacket, shirt, pants socks, shoes; carrying a black canvas bad and sunglasses coupled with a New York attitude.

- Some fashion statements are just annoying. Take "body piercing". If you're not a masochist, what the hell kind of statement are you making by sticking a needle through a sensitive part of your body. "Look! I pierced my nipples, tongue, nose and eye lids. I'm so cool, and your not if it bothers you!" During winter, these people must be real tense if they're at a party where the host is showing off a new deep pile carpet. All you need is one slightly drunk guy shuffling his feet. **ZZZZZIT!**

- Women catch hell in the fashion industry. One year it's skinny, next year voluptuous. Big hair, short hair. And look at the controversy over the female breast! <u>Before</u> the Dow Chemical scandal, every mother's daughter screamed bloody murder that implants were immoral, unnatural, a cheat, a sick fantasy fulfillment for men! But I didn't hear one peep when some designer creates a swimsuit with built in inflatable falsies, or these cleavage creating wonder bras. So stuffing 'em with plastic like a Christmas turkey until they stand up like a balloon in the Macy's Day Parade is wrong. But tying, squeezing and pushing 'em together until they look like two bald headed men trying to wear one sweater is OK. Sounds like a sick plot for a bondage movie at the Trench Coat Theater to me. "You can't escape me, girlie! Now I'll just truss up them boobs with a little device of my own design. HEH, HEH!!"

- Hair styles change with the frequency of a cheap shortwave radio. When I was little kid, 60's revolution changed black folks hairstyle from short and/or greased to the AFRO. Man, by Senior High I had 7 inches bouncing on my head, mustache, beard and a steel hair rake (used as a weapon in some parts of the world) ripping a hole in my back pocket. That was cool then. There was that Gerri Curl period, but that stopped when six people caught fire at a Teddy Pendigrass concert in '81. Now, kids have everything from their social security numbers etched on the back of their heads to a square box of hair smack in the middle of a bald head.

I may change my hair style, but I REFUSE to change from a barber shop to a hair stylist. Why? Simple. If my barber screws up, I can get pissed off only so much. After all, what can you expect for $12 (including tip). But if I spend $45 dollars to have some clown of unknown sexual orientation dance on my head for an hour with shampoos, blow dryers and what have you, while listening to the coffee klatch conversation with "the girls"; and my hair is still messed up, SOMEBODY IS GOING TO GET HURT.

<u>Irritations</u>

- No matter what the ethnic or racial background, it seems common practice for a recent immigrant family that owns a salad bar or magazine shop to place the relative with the least understanding of the English language in the most strategic aspect of the business; the cash register or the Lotto machine. Response to a question like, "Do you have this..." is a blank stare like a deer caught in car headlights.

-    Preparing for a important event: showering, shaving, brushing your teeth, putting on your best clothes.  Then suddenly having to evacuate those burritos from last night's dinner.

-    Being in the company of people that you're really trying to impress, and having to hold in a very persistent case of flatulence.  The fog horn kind.

-    Yearly physical examinations for men:  Wearing those stupid rear-view smocks and paper shoes while walking down freezing, crowded hallways; your naked butt sticking to the deli sandwich paper covering the exam table; waiting forever in a cold room for the doctor to return "in a few minutes"; trying to ignore an intense erection when the well-built nurse takes your temperature and pulse; trying to get rid of the same erection when a female doctor walks in an announces she'll be filling in for your old, male doctor during the **full examination** part.

-    Being the only single employee in an office filled with older, homely and/or horny, married co-workers of the opposite sex.

-    Bragging about a restaurant you found 2 months ago to your new date, and arriving there to find it was closed by the Board of Health 1 month ago.

-    Having a bad case of feet the night the host of the dinner party announces, "Let's all just kick off our shoes and relax!"

-    The price of a postage stamp.  This 2 cents here, 3 cents next year bullshit.  Does a mugger come up to you and say, "Gimme a third of your money", then follows you several blocks and says, "OK, now gimme the rest".?

-    People quizzing a visitor from a foreign country like they're a U.N. envoy.  If this person is like a typical American, they work 9 to 5, watch the sports or entertainment channel, and read their equivalent of the New York Post.  In other words, they don't know a damn thing that's going on in their country either!

-    Chronic smokers in denial:  Look, <u>occasionally</u> enjoying a good cigar after an expensive meal, <u>occasionally</u> lighting a pipe to enjoy with a good book or a cigarette with a drink and friends is **smoking for pleasure.**  Standing in 40 degree, rainy, wind swept weather, hunched over in the crevice of some building during lunch time sucking on a cigarette butt is an **ADDICTION, OK?**

-    Commuters to Manhattan who refuse to wear complete winter clothing.  It's 30 degrees, windy with snow flurries.  They wear only a business suit, maybe gloves, hat and a scarf.  Why?  Because the "true commuter" is only exposed to the elements a total of 15 minutes a day (driven to the train station, subway from Grand Central or Penn station, a two block walk to the office).  So why wear that heavy weather gear?  Because it only takes 5 minutes of exposure to kick off influenza.  These same people wonder what spreads the cold season ever year.  You do, Asshole.

-    Female body builders with cro-magnon jaws, no necks, breast totally receded into pectoral muscle, arms bigger than most men's legs and bass-like voices; claiming they don't use any artificial supplements and they do this to themselves "to look and feel the best they can".

-    The person you see at the supermarket and fantasized about decides to engage you in conversation AND tell you they're single – the one day you decide picking up a quart of milk wouldn't require brushing your teeth, combing your hair, or wearing decent looking clothes.

-    A dentist of exceptional, almost painless skill, great personality, and breath that repels mosquitoes for 12 yards.

-    Introducing your 5 year old child/brother/sister to people.  Just after you've bragged about how smart and well behaved they are, the kid decides to dig a booger out of their nose with the stretching properties of silly putty.


The Little Things in Life

-    Observe the jay walker during rush hour.  See them give drivers a bad look and defiantly walk slower when they're honked at.  These people are obviously not aware of the laws of probability.  In my book, the chances of a fit, 200 pound man winning a fight with an edgy, wimpy 140 pound smaller man sitting in a 2 Ton automobile are less than zero.

-    Congressmen announcing that there will be no more money for this or that; usually after a State dinner that cost more than the monthly budget for a local school.

-    Actors/Actresses adamantly denying any real sexual feelings during a torrid love scene.  "It's just acting, "they say.  Yeah, when they claim that bit of science fiction it's acting.  Now I'm a red blooded heterosexual American male.  If I'm in a bed with a beautiful naked woman whose fondling and kissing me, I'm damn sure going to be pointing due to north without my hands.  Most likely the director yells, "…and cut.  I said CUT.  HEY!  CUT IT OUT, DAMMIT!"

-    New York cab drivers that have 1 major problem with the English language.  "It's drive DE-fensively guys, NOT Of-fensively.

-    It's amazing how men become irresistible to the opposite sex the moment after they become engaged.  Guys you know personally who were lucky to get laid once every 2 years suddenly have to beat them off with a stick.  And you might as well get acquainted with your right hand, because no one is giving you the time of day while you stand next to them.  Another aspect of this phenomena is the resurrection of the "ex-flame".  You know, the woman you were crazy about who suddenly dumped you?  It takes years to get over her, and finally meet a great new girl.  And during the first time you make love, the doorbell rings.  Lo and behold, it's the ex-flame, replete in a killer Teddy and carrying a bottle of wine.  "Hi, I was just thinking about you! Are you busy?"

-    Parents who relate to their children like they're both on God damned Sesame Street discussing uses of the letter A.  They usually do this on a commuter train or bus, the one your trying to get some sleep on after a particularly bad day at work. (loud, staged voice) "Why yes Janey, that's correct.  My, aren't we clever!  Now what other uses can we think of for adverbs, Hmmm?!?"  This is why I thank God for gun control laws.

-    It is now legal in New York City for women to go bare chested in public during hot summer days as long as they don't "act in a lewd and lascivious manner."  Why do I have the sneaking suspicion that the only women who'll take advantage of this will be the ones that you do not want to see topless?

- Isn't it comforting to know that the guys you grew up with who got any woman they wanted, and treated them like door mats, are now married to a cranky wives, with three daughters and have solid grey hair before they're 40.

- Chance reunion with old junior high school teachers: they compliment you on how nice you turned out and how they always new you had potential, blah, blah. And all you remember are the detentions and trips to the principals office. Then you remember what you vowed on graduation day you would do to this clown if you ever met them in the adult world. But you can't (it's called assault with intent to kill). Just take comfort in the fate that they're now old as dirt and will soon croak.

- The request by New York Traffic Patrol (those wonderful green suited folks) to carry fire arms. By all means, let us give the city's most irritating, short tempered, narrow minded public employees the ability to shoot civilians for having the audacity to park their cars and ask outrageous questions like, "What sign?"

- Remember when proposing the wealthy to pay an equal percentage of taxes with the rest of the country was denounced as "soaking the rich"? How the rich screamed that because of the luxury tax "The yacht construction industry would be ruined" putting several thousand craftsman out of work? I doubt that the folks who work at your local coffee shop (up before dawn, home after dark) are upset that Wodsworth and Cecily won't be able to yacht to Cancun, or the yacht construction folks will have to lower themselves to building affordable fishing boats.

- The uncanny ability of small children to control their bladders. You watch them on Saturday morning consume 2 bowls of cereal, 2 pints of grape juice and remain paralyzed in front of the TV for 4 consecutive hours. Yet, deprived of all liquids for 24 hours, during the sudden death play of the Super Bowl, those dreaded 8 words; **"I haf' ta go to da bat twoom".**

- Interviews with TV talk shows hosts, who talk about the social relevance of their interaction with the audience, how sections of society can benefit from watching problems being openly discussed and resolved, etc., etc. Then you read the TV guide description of the next show's topic, "Big Busted Porn Stars Who Leave Their Husbands for Their Reverend's Teen Son".

- Finally giving in and going to a family reunion function. You know you're going to meet that one elderly relative who's going to reminisce about how you pissed on Santa Claus's leg at age 6. They'll do this in front of distant relatives to whom you're only related to by marriage and have no idea who you are.

<u>…And the correct answer is:</u>

- Television is flooded with diet and exercise info-mericials showing people who claim a "hereditary" inability to lose weight, or absolutely no time to work out. Here is a simple, cost effective solution: During the summer, blindfold these folks, then drop them off stark naked and empty handed in a vast wilderness area for a week or so. I guarantee not only will they be slimmed down when you pick them up, but they'll be able to do a 6 minute mile every time you turn out the lights and growl like a bear.

- Instead of lobbying capitol hill, have married and single working parents drop their kids off at the house of their local congressional representatives who want to cut day care funding. Clear all that nonsense up real quick!

- The worst musicians, poets, artists, or for that matter human beings in the world need no longer fear unemployment. Get a NEA grant and rich people will feed you, give you money and treat you like the second coming. That's why the new Republican Congress wants to shut the NEA down. They figure if anyone is going to be a federally funded asshole, it should be only them.

- Rather than waste time and money debating prayer in public schools, just have the teachers announce a surprise test every morning; on a different subject each day. It's a sure bet the students will start each sentence with "OH GOD, please help me!"

- Totally eliminate the military. Instead, have personal training centers for politicians and anyone else who feels war is a solution. Then, you put these people together in a dark room armed only with baseball bats. While this is happening, the rest of us learn to share and be nice to each other.

- Forget all this nonsense about sex education, condoms, etc. for teenagers. To ensure that teenagers will not engage in pre-marital sex, just show them a hidden camera video of their parents doing the wild thing. Not only will you stop teen sex, but you'll guarantee therapists years of future employment.

- The cure for Ronald Reagan's alzheimer affliction: Run him for President again. That way the Great Communicator will once again be perfectly alright, and never make any serious mistakes worth mentioning. Just like he did for 8 years.

- Final solution to what is the true religion: Have representatives from various faiths and denominations compete in a "miracle contest" on the Oprah Winfrey show. First person to perform a true physical miracle, like making Oprah vanish from television, gets to claim world theological dominance.

- Do you really want separation of Church and State? OK, make them pay full taxes like everyone else. It'll be pretty hard trying to control other people's sexual morals and conduct when they're getting fucked by the IRS.


It's Understandable

- … for the slow progress of medical science: a woman doctor stands before some prestigious AMA board to explain her revolutionary new life saving diagnostic technique, and the first thoughts of the male board members are, "Is it the jacket or are her tits really that big?"

- … that there is a significant rise in violent behavior by today's youth: the most popular national past time is watching grown men beat each other senseless over an oblong piece of inflated leather. This is not only a game, but (legend has it) the sport has the ability to "build character and teach discipline to be applied to all aspects of life". Question; when was the last time you rammed your shoulder into someone's gut during a job interview?

-    … that people do not trust most elected officials.  When the person fighting for your financial interest on Capitol Hill was born into a rich family, and has investments in the corporation that just shut down your place of employment, chances are their not exactly "your" congressional representative.

-    … for people to be a little paranoid.  Just think, the kids who you called "geeks" and "nerds" in high school and college became computer jocks.  They can now control your financial life with a push of a few buttons.  And you wonder why they always show at the Reunions.  Perhaps,… to KEEP TABS ON YOU?!?

-    … that parents of today's teenagers can't stand their music.  After all, the music and lyrics of the Sixties was much more intense and complex with depth and meaning, like "..MACEO!  HIT MEH!  UNNGH!"

<u>Did You Ever Notice...</u>
by Vincent Jenkins


... that the people who occupy health stores are generally unhealthy looking?  No matter how much wheat grass juice, herbal extracts, and bean curds they stuff themselves with, they are still the wimpiest looking people on the face of the Earth.  Maybe they should put down the East meditation books, get off their scrawny asses and play some basketball.  And an occasional Whopper, fries and milk shake wouldn't hurt either.

... that the middle and upper middle class will bitch and moan when a working stiff uses the system to get a few extra bucks?  But check out how fast they clam up when the rich screw the tax system through bullshit loopholes.  Case in point; a toll booth worker logs in record overtime to inflate his retirement pension, and local newspapers are calling for his blood.  Yet Chrysler Motors produces defective Tanks for the military, gets nailed for it, declares bankruptcy, lays off thousands of workers and starts all over, and is hailed as an industrial/economic leader.  Listen up people, a guy who sucks gas fumes to collect money for the state deserves a break.  Lee Iacocca, for screwing the American public by making a bad product and punishing others for it deserves a break across his neck.

... that the only program on commercial television that acknowledges human defecation is "Married with Children"?  A bizarre, mean spirited, cynical little comedy is the only place where a necessary human function is included in it's repertoire.  Just once, I would like to see a character in a soap opera say, "You're too young to marry him Martha!  You have no idea how this news upsets me.  We'll finish this discussion after I take a dump."

... how totally insipid the questions are for these Beauty Pageant finalist?  Usually, the question is something like "And how would you use your title to benefit mankind?"  Now really! In front of millions of TV viewers, is the contestant going to truthfully answer, "Mankind hasn't done shit for me baby.  I'm getting paid and laid for this gig!

... how people will bad mouth you if your clothes are slightly wrinkled or out of date, or if your apartment is slightly cluttered.  These same people will buy a hot dog from a street vendor without a second thought.  It has been documented by numerous newspaper and TV reports that most vending carts and the hot dogs are kept in warehouses that should be condemned by the Board of Health; street people who have forgotten what soap and water is are employed to prepare the "fix ins" that go on the food (as well as clean the carts, using the filthy rag du jour). So the next time some jerk thinks they're a rep from Good Housekeeping and gives you a hard time, you know where to but them lunch.
... the universal disease which affects the memory of all parents when their children become adults?  Suddenly, their minds connect with a past that can only exist in fairy tales, a world where they never were cranky, made bad judgements, or treated their children like total idiots during the teenage years.  By the same token, the adult children remember themselves as innocent victims of oppressive parents.  That their experiments with pre-marital sex, drugs & alcohol use, and secret road trips were totally innocent and explainable.  These are classic cases of denial that would give any psychologist cause to put down payment on a Porsche.

.. that babies will throw a fit that can only be stopped by you handing them an important personal item?  No matter what favorite toy is at hand, most toddlers shut their yaps only when you hand them your expensive wristwatch, jewelry or new eye glasses.  After their little hands have pounded the object into an interesting new shape, they toss it aside and crawl happily away.

This is the basis for what is now know as "primal scream" therapy, because that's what parents do when they see the result of junior's work.

... that people with truly horrific breath are extremely long winded individuals? From their perspective, it's normal that all people frown when being talked to. Also, frowning must mean to them that some folks are hard of hearing. So instead of speaking up, they move in closer. How they explain the listener's crying, feinting, or screaming and running away is a mystery to me.

... the hypocritical attitude this society had towards the common working man and woman? Praised on one hand as the backbone of America, they are the butt of every sitcom joke on television. An example: spunky secretary bullshits her way into a ritzy party for the well-to-do. She thinks she has met her wealthy, handsome dream date, only to later discover that he's actually a night manager at White Castle! Now as I see it, there is nothing funny about slinging burgers at 2 a.m. for any simpleton with a buck. Nor is it humorous that the hamburger jockey comparatively pays **more taxes** than a corporate junior executive. So next time you want to laugh at a TV show that makes fun of a garbage man, try hauling your own crud in the truck of **your car** to the city dump.

... (**for men**) that you're the only person at a pool party who has trouble concealing his erection? Every other man can be wearing a French bikini brief, slow dance with stunning string bikini'ed women and will be barely poking out. Meanwhile, from just talking to one of these women, your swimsuit (which looks like your grandfather's boxer shorts) resembles a Boy Scout pup-tent.

... the uncanny ability of people to suddenly "need" items that are destined for the garbage heap? Examples are: The beat up, cruddy looking old toy you found during spring cleaning in the back of the closet suddenly becomes the psychological pin that will unhinge your five year old if he finds out you tossed it; the pair of ratty, hole punched underwear that window penis and buttocks becomes your husband's "perfect fit" when he sees the new expensive pairs you've bought in the clothes drawer; that terrible looking jacket your wife bought you during courtship. It's collected dust in the closet, and just as you're about to donate it to the Salvation Army, you must wear it to your 20th high school reunion (because your ex-flame will be there). This need is usually followed by the ultimatum "if you really loved me you wouldn't have even thought of throwing it away!"

... that no matter how much effort companies put into simplifying rules, regulations and insurance coverage for all of it's employees; people will still depend upon the one or two individuals who actually read the material to explain it. Seminars, conferences, and hot lines will not prevent this phenomena. It's like spending serious dollars to get your kid the latest in toy technology for Christmas, only to have them play "fort building" with the cardboard boxes the stuff came in.

... people who hold up the line at fast food restaurants while trying to make decisions during the lunch hour? These folk act like they're ordering their last meal with questions like "Can I have extra cheese instead of pickles and onions? And what would that cost? What's its taste like?" Don't you just want to scream, **"IT'S A FUCKING HAMBURGER, FOR CHRIST SAKES. JUST BUY ONE TODAY AND IF YOU DON'T LIKE IT YOU CAN HAVE MINE!!!"**

... how some people will nearly go into shock upon spotting their favorite television/movie star on the street? "My God," they say. "He/She looks terrible! Look at how he/she's let him/her self go!  Boy, does he/she look old!  It never occurs to these folks that (a) the movie they admired these celebrities is at least 20 years old.  (b) movies are not real.  People are made up to look different.  (c) Real people get old (d) if they check themselves out in old photo, then in the mirror, they may not be so quick to criticize.

… that the relatives that you can **least tolerate** are always the ones with the **most money** to leave in their wills?

… how weird the sexual organs of man and woman look?  Honestly, wouldn't they look better in painting done by Picasso on a weekend drunk rather than attached to your body?  Obviously, God did some last minute work on the 6th day at 5 minutes to quitt'in time.

… the insidious evil of the credit card?  Every time you qualify for a new credit card you answer you'll only use it **when absolutely necessary.**  And you know God damn well that you'll use it to spend money like there's no tomorrow!  Why?  As a famous man once said, "Because it's there!"

… that the promoters for "Butt of Bronze," "Stomach of Steel," and other similar exercise products are all former world class athletes or professional trainers?  Get real people!  Working up a sweat with some plastic and chrome contraption alone is not going to get you a body like the sponsor.  More likely, you'll get a "Wallet of Poverty" from buying this stuff.  And while we're on the subject, will somebody explain to me why Bruce Jenner got a face job that makes him look like a weasel?  Does he think a pinched, beaky face will actually increase sales?  Wake up Bruce, it ain't happening!

… that no matter how much money the State Lottery generates, the legislators always claim a deficit in the very same programs that the Lottery was set to supplement?  Even with the occasional big winner, millions of dollars are collected by the Lottery on a weekly basis.  Now the question is not where is the money, but which state employees vacation in Tahiti.

… how kids can be terrified by the dark of their room, yet want to ride every "Spook House" ride at the Amusement Park?  How the same kid has to be gassed during a routine cleaning at the dentist, and yet come home dirty, bloody, and smiling with two teeth missing yelling "I juth made the pee-wee foothball theam!"

… that whenever there's a summer water shortage declared by the local government, private golf courses in the area mysteriously remain lush and green?  Everyone gets their water from the same place, yet whole you're taking 2 minute showers, those 18 hole course sprinkles spritz away every day for at least half an hour.  Now I seriously doubt golf clubs have 1000 gallon storage tanks in case of hot, dry weather.  Most likely the club management has stored away a few bucks in the pocket of the Dept. of Water supervisor an other local politicians (who just happen to be members).

… that there are no Surgeon General warnings on the packaging of junk food?  In the last 10 years the American public has been swamped with information on the health hazards of our environment and diet.  The Twinky snack cake is a known felon in the war on sugar, cholesterol, and fat.  Yet all the rotund 12 year old sees is a box with a cartoon on the front and some meaningless stats in small print.  Mind you, if the box read "WARNING!  THE SURGEON GENERAL HAS DETERMINED THAT THIS FOODSTUFF CAN PROMOTE A FAT ASS", I think sales would drop considerably.

… that the guys who cram into their local bar for "Wet T-Shirt Night" freak out when an attractive woman decides to nurse her baby in public?  Damned if I can explain it.

… how famous actors go to great lengths to separate themselves from their adoring fans (You and Me)?  When they say "I love my fans" its usually from some secluded place where you and I couldn't afford a glass of seltzer, let alone live there.  The next time you watch "Lifestyles of the Rich and Famous" just remember that it was your $7 that help buy them that private beach in the Bahamas that you'll never see in your lifetime.

…the bizarre learning habits of children?  Your kid just can't grasp the concept of <u>neatly</u> dressing themselves before going out to play.  Or they have problems retaining school lessons after 6 months of repetition.  But from viewing a 30 second commercial <u>just once</u>, they have a photographic detailing of what toy to buy, it's accessories, how to put it together, the name, history, and 6 store outlets near you (with directions) that the toy is distributed at.